TRUSTING THE INSCRUTABLE WAYS OF PROVIDENCE

Trusting the Inscrutable Ways of Providence

GEORGE WASHINGTON'S SPIRITUAL PATH TO JOY

The Rev. Dr. Lynn Ronaldi

Lynn P. Ronaldi

With Gratitude to God,
this Book is Dedicated with Love to:

The Communion of Saints at Pohick Church
on its 250th Anniversary, 1774-2024

And Especially to my Beloved Family:
Tom, Alley, Tori and Carly Ronaldi

Table of Contents

Acknowledgements

Trusting in the Inscrutable Ways of Providence: George Washington's Spiritual Path to Joy was a spark that kindled when I arrived at Pohick Church in 2018 and became 16th Rector of Washington's home church.

In those first days, I admit I was a bit starstruck at our colonial church's illustrious spiritual ancestors, among them Washington as well as George Mason, George Fairfax and other prominent families. Pohickians graciously embraced my fervor as I preached about them several times that year. Those early sermons glorified our ancestors as exemplary icons of faith, pillars of perfection, models to be imitated.

I became particularly intrigued with the faith of George Washington. And, as I dove more deeply into researching his life, original writings, and histories by several authors, my perception of him gradually changed. My understanding of his spiritual contribution evolved, becoming more realistic than idealistic. I began to see him as an imperfect human who wrestled with inner struggles – and opened himself to transformation.

I was more impressed with Washington's flawed humanity than I was with his hallowed character. The more I learned about his spiritual formation, my urgency to share Washington's true and lasting gift fanned into flame.

I was convinced that Washington should neither be placed on a pillar nor demonized. Rather, subsequent generations should emulate him for his honest struggles, his evolving faith, and his lifelong process of transformation.

His story is inspiring precisely because his journey to joy wasn't a straight path. It involved inner conflict, setbacks, and suffering. Yet he stayed in the struggle. He learned to embrace both the *"cup of suffering"* and the *"cup of blessing."* Near the end of his life, he made difficult choices and arrived at an integrity and dependence on God that led to genuine *"happiness."*

Washington ultimately encountered a deep well of trust in God's mysterious ways. Regardless of life's circumstances, he had learned to surrender to, and depend on God, whom he called *"Providence."*

As a mature adult, Washington would often indirectly allude to St. Paul's letter to the Romans (Chapter 11:33-36), as he described his trust in God's unsearchable ways. He used variations of the phrase, *"trusting in the inscrutable ways of Providence"* at least 25 times. [1] One quote was recorded in his letter to Colonel Basset in April 1773:

> *"The ways of Providence being inscrutable, and the justice of it not to be scanned by the shallow eye of humanity, nor to be counteracted by utmost efforts of human power and wisdom, resignation, and as far as the strength of our reason and religion carry us, a cheerful acquiescence to the Divine Will, is what we are to aim."*[2]

I am thankful to have been invited to pore over books and online resources in the George Washington Presidential Library at nearby Mount Vernon. Over the span of a few years, I have had access to an abundance of material on colonial religion and Washington's life and faith.

Brilliant historians and scholars at Mount Vernon, Dr. Doug Bradburn, Dr. Patrick Spero, and Dr. Mary Thompson, allowed me to bounce ideas off them. They encouraged me and directed me to sources. I had the honor of sitting on a symposium panel with renowned authors Dr. Richard Newman and Dr. John Fea.

None of my curiosity would have borne fruit without those who helped form me spiritually. I give undying thanks for the prayerful example of my beloved mother, Jan Alley Petrie, and my treasured spiritual directors, Sister Adeline O'Donoghue and The Rev. Martin Smith. In addition to my immediate family, whom I thank below, I am grateful for my grandparents, father, sisters, extended family and in-laws, especially my mother in law Iris Hope Ronaldi

I am also thankful for inspiring professors Dr. Judy Ryan, The Rev. Dr. Julia Gatta, and The Rev. Dr. Ben King. I thank the Bishops who have believed in me, especially The Rt. Rev. Duncan Gray III, who ordained me and encouraged me to pursue doctoral studies. I am also grateful for Benedictine formation in the Community of Hope International. Scripture and several spiritual authors and contemplative theologians continue to enrich my spiritual journey.

I thank friends and encouragers The Rev. Sandra DePriest, Kathleen Merchant, Susan Telling, Karen Clifton, Kathe Clark, Lisa Lubiani, Cissy Connelly, The Rev. Catherine Tatem, The Rev. Dr. Doug Travis, Father Scott James and The Rev. Dr. Al Carden. I am also grateful for Pohick friends D'Andrea and Michael Wooten, Micheyl and Jim Bartholomew, Mike and Julie Elston, Dick Hamly, Beth Altman, Mari Harding, Judy Schmid, the Herberts, Kniplings,

Nelsons, Remalys, Bontragers, Abrams, Leons, Bradburns, Browns, Bergers, Bireleys and Greathouses – and countless other Pohickians – for their loving support. Thank you to all of Pohick's outstanding Vestry and Staff, and especially this book's graphic artist and editor Deborah Hennig; cover illustrator and typesetter Rach Johnson; and Pohickian Jackie Wells, whose original sketch of Pohick Church is included. Also thanks to Samantha Snyder and Dana Steffanelli of the George Washington Presidential Library for helping with research and proofreading. I am grateful for the encouragement and support of the Mount Vernon Ladies' Association.

Most of all, I thank my husband and best friend Tom Ronaldi for his undying love, wisdom, encouragement, patience, and humor, as well as our incredibly warm, brilliant, beautiful, fun and loving daughters-who-are-also-best friends: Alley, Tori and Carly, and their significant others.

I especially dedicate this book to my husband Tom and to our daughters.

I also dedicate this book to all Pohickians, past, present and future.

A Tribute to Pohick Church

Sketch by Pohick Church parishioner Jackie Wells.

This book about George Washington's spiritual formation was written in honor of Pohick Church on the occasion of its 250th Jubilee Celebration. It is a tribute to the saints at Pohick Church – past, present and future.

Originally called the "Occoquan Church," Pohick Church was the seat of Truro Parish, where Washington's father Augustine was elected to its vestry (board of elders) in 1735, just three years after George's birth.

In those days, a "parish" was a geographic area similar to a today's "county." Pre-Revolution parish boundaries were established by the Church of England and consisted of a group of churches in that area. A parish's function was both spiritual and temporal. A church was used both for worship and for community gathering.

Pohick was generally regarded as the "Mother Church of Northern Virginia." It is believed to have derived its name from a Native American word for "hickory tree."

Augustine Washington remained a Pohickian the rest of his life. He introduced his young son George to Pohick Church. The church was initially housed in a wooden building on Old Colchester Road near Occoquan Bay, about six to seven miles from Mount Vernon.

In 1761, at age 29, George Washington was elected to the Truro Parish vestry at Pohick, and he remained there for 23 years! Shortly afterward, in 1763, Washington was elected Pohick's vestry warden (presider). He held that leadership position until he left for military service in 1775. He did not resign from Pohick's vestry until the end of the Revolutionary War, in 1784.[3]

During those 23 years when Washington was active on Pohick's vestry, he was formed not only in church leadership, but also in community leadership. Under the umbrella of the Church of England and subjects of the English crown, a vestry also functioned as magistrates for the surrounding region, or Truro Parish.

In addition to calling a Rector (priest with canonical authority over the parish) and managing the practical needs of the church, the vestry was tasked with collecting taxes (called "tithes), managing a glebe of farmland to support the community, making some decisions on justice, and caring for widows and orphans.

During that era, Pohick Church not only housed worship services; it also accommodated community meetings. Likely, one of the first places both the *Fairfax Resolves* and the *Declaration of Independence* were read was on the steps of Pohick.

During those years on Pohick's vestry, he was exposed to the Anglican *via media,* or middle way. At Pohick, young Washington was formed as a measured, prayerful, reasonable, and moderate leader.

During Washington's years as warden, the Vestry Minutes indicate that Pohick's leaders became concerned about the deteriorating condition of the original wooden church. The vestry determined that a brick structure should take its place.

It was reported that Washington and his friend George Mason sparred over where to relocate Pohick Church; the Vestry Minutes describe the debate as a "warm" one. Washington advocated for a site closer to Mount Vernon; Mason was just fine with the current location, just a couple of miles from his home, Gunston Hall.

Washington used his surveying skills to recommend a site for the new building. He made the case for a location that would meet the needs of a growing demographic – and one that happened to be a little closer to Mount Vernon, on the Mount Vernon side of Pohick Creek. Washington's carefully constructed argument won the day.

Washington, Mason, and George Fairfax, among other notable patriots, helped design and build the "new Pohick Church." The new church opened its doors for worship in 1774, just two years before the Declaration of Independence was signed.

That sturdy brick Georgian structure remains today at the corner of Old Colchester Road and Richmond Highway – a testament to its founders' faith formation. Today, Pohick Church is the spiritual home of a large, lively, and hospitable congregation.

The following chapters trace Washington's path of transformation through various eras of his life. It begins with the earliest seeds of Washington's Christian formation, sown by his family. The Washingtons raised their children with devout prayer, Scripture study, and moral education.

Those roots grew deeper and wider through regular Anglican (Church of England) formation and worship, which included weekly immersion in Scripture and Anglican liturgy. His regular attendance in Anglican services meant he was regularly exposed to the sacraments of Baptism and the Holy Eucharist, and to readings from Holy Scripture,

Growing up in the established Church of England, Washington was formed in the Anglican *"via media,"* or *"middle way."* This was an ethos of moderation, civility, morality, and breadth.

Throughout his life, Washington learned and recited Scripture; practiced servant leadership; participated in Communion in the pre-war days; soaked in the Anglican ethos of moderation and balance; and formed a deep and abiding belief in religious tolerance.

Even so, Washington's spiritual life was no straight shot, no arrow piercing heaven's bulls-eye on day one! Like most of us, he wrestled with his own inner landscape and with questions of suffering and evil along the way.

Washington dealt with grief and loss, physical hardship, heartbreaking decisions, moral dilemmas, and defeat. Yet even in the midst of his greatest struggles, he never lost hope. His evolving trust in what he called the *"inscrutable ways of Providence,"* his perseverance on the spiritual journey, helped form him into what biographers universally describe as the greatest American statesman ever.

> *"Objective evidence for asserting that George Washington deserves the premier position among all American statesmen is overwhelming,"* biographer Peter Henriques writes. *"He was unanimously elected commander in chief of the Continental Army, unanimously elected president of the Constitutional Convention, unanimously elected first President of the United States, and unanimously re-elected. George Washington was truly 'America's Indispensable Man...People today forget how close the American experiment came to failure and extinction...during its vulnerable years, he guided a disparate group of states toward nationhood... George Washington was critical in preventing the collapse of the whole endeavor."* [4]

Even though the world recognizes George Washington's vision, achievements and indisputable contribution to the Great Experiment of democracy, this book addresses his struggles and losses as well. It examines how his faith was formed in the midst of them.

These chapters trace his very human, lifelong process of spiritual formation, much of which occurred in the context of a tolerant, moderate Anglican (Church of England) ethos and theology. A lifelong process of prayer, humble self-reflection, and a willingness to be changed, transformed Washington into the great wisdom figure he is universally believed to be.

Washington's life was not easy. The path was never a straight line. He experienced a normal process of formation, and growth.

Washington's faith evolved over time, from a simple yet grounded childhood faith, to maturation -- through the struggles of young adulthood, the losses of middle age, and the joys and regrets of old age.

Through every stage and each life experience, Washington was gradually transformed into a genuine wisdom figure grounded in a mature and abiding faith and known for his integrity of life.

Readers may notice how various stages of Washington's spiritual journey mirror aspects of their own, and are encouraged to reflect on stages of their own spiritual journeys.

Early in life, Washington's childlike faith was grounded in prayer and scripture. He experienced a great loss at an early age that changed him: the death of his father. Doubtless, he felt a keen responsibility for his mother, Mary Ball Washington, and his siblings.

Next, he moved through a period of young adulthood, in which he believed he could win battles with God's sure blessing.

Later, as a full-fledged adult, the young Pohick Church vestryman was formed in a broad-minded, latitudinarian ethos of Anglican spirituality and church leadership. That ethos surely helped mold his passion for freedom of religious tolerance, unity, and liberty in pursuit of happiness.

Some historians argue that Washington was not a Christian. This book firmly supports the contention that Washington was Christian in many ways. For instance, prior to the Revolutionary War, Washington's family and others reported that he attended Eucharists regularly. He seemed particularly moved by the Anglican "beauty of holiness" as he helped design and outfit the new Pohick Church. As vestryman, he purchased a leatherbound, corporate Book of Common Prayer for worship, which Pohick still possesses today.

According to Pohick's original vestry minutes now kept in Mount Vernon's George Washington Presidential Library, Washington also ordered a beautiful gold-gilt-lettered reredos (altar backing) for Pohick Church. The reredos includes the 10 commandments, the Lord's Prayer, and the Apostles Creed – all of which proclaim a Trinitarian faith and belief in Jesus' death and resurrection.

Later, when Washington was elevated to General and Commander in Chief in the Revolutionary War, his faith was tried and tested by dire circumstances. In the midst of failure and heartache, he frequently used Eucharistic language to describe the *"Cup of Suffering."* Even though he began to abstain from partaking in communion during this phase – for reasons that shall be discussed -- his faith deepened substantially.

As first President of the United States, Washington commended and modeled a life of prayer, moderation, and gratitude as the very basis for both individual and national *"Happiness."* He was also an ardent proponent of the Freedom of Religion. He was adamant that every individual should worship based on his or her own conscience.

Ultimately, near the end of his presidency and during his golden years at Mount Vernon, George attained a level of peace and a hard-earned wisdom. He was convicted that a nation that was void of prayer, that placed restrictions on freedom, or that engaged in division that polarizes, would never experience *"Happiness."*

The pinnacle of George's lasting spiritual legacy was his insistence that both personal and national joy, or happiness, must be rooted and grounded in union with God and others. During his golden years, he often uses the Eucharistic phrase, *"Cup of Blessing"* to describe this sense of joy.

Over his lifetime, Washington faced many of life's greatest challenges – more than some of us will ever experience. Yet, grounded in prayer, humble self-reflection, and an openness to his own transformation, Washington gradually grew into a wise, mature trust in God -- regardless of life's circumstances.

In contemplating the progression of Washington's spiritual formation, and his embrace of both the *"cup of suffering"* and the *"cup of blessing,"* perhaps the reader will discover, or rediscover, that deep-seated well of Christian hope and joy, which George Washington so often described as *"happiness."*

This exploration of Washington's formation will make his spiritual legacy more accessible and inspiring. Washington's relatable journey will encourage readers to persevere in prayer, struggle and change through honest self-reflection, and grow in integrity.

1

Introduction

When one imagines our first President, the picture that often comes to mind is a solemn face that rarely smiles. On one extreme, history portrays George Washington as a stiff and solemn moral icon, an untouchable man of such strong character that he is practically a saint. On the other extreme, some historians seek to discredit his faith.

Yet thousands of letters and diary entries, as well as first-hand eyewitness accounts of his life, point to this conclusion: George Washington maintained a lifelong relationship with God, whom he called "Providence." He also believed in Jesus Christ, to whom he alluded as *"The Divine Author of our Faith."*

Washington was neither a perfect person, nor was he a moral failure. One should neither idolize nor demonize him. Washington's greatest gifts to us may have in fact been his spiritual and moral struggles, his willingness to be transformed over the span of a lifetime, and his evolving trust in what he called *"the inscrutable ways of Providence."*

"Providence" was a word many in his day used for God. Like the psalmist who wrote Psalm 139, Washington gradually came to see that God was unknowable, or as he describes God's ways, *"inscrutable."* In time, Washington also came to believe we could trust God's ways, even in the face of suffering and evil.

This trust in God's ways regardless of suffering and pain was not always present in his life. As a youth, he lacked wisdom; his prayer life was proscribed and simple.

As a young man fighting in the French and Indian War, Washington lacked experience and realistic vision. He believed in God's presence and action only when things went well for him. When his life was spared, he naively presumed he was in God's favor.

As a family man and churchman, Washington was formed in leadership at his home church, Pohick Church. His father Augustine had served on Pohick's vestry, and likewise, George served on that vestry for 23 of his formative years: from the age of 29, in 1761, to the age of 52, in 1784.

Later, as a General of the Continental Army -- when he faced suffering, sickness, death, and near despair over the cause -- Washington's faith deepened considerably. From his correspondence and diaries it is clear that he wrestled with the problem of suffering and evil. In the midst of the trials and tribulations of war, he persevered in prayer. He ordered his troops to pray- and according to their own religious tradition.

Throughout all the various periods of his life, Washington experienced a normal human journey of spiritual formation, including struggles, setbacks, and new beginnings.

Along the way, Washington learned to characterize the mystery of God at work in his life as *"the inscrutable ways of Providence."* Over his lifetime, Washington gradually grew into the moral exemplar and faith icon whose ideals and actions helped shape a new and *"happy"* nation.

Yet, Washington did not become that exemplar overnight. One need not keep him on a spiritual pedestal. On closer examination, his actual journey is much more complicated, relatable and inspiring. Like most human spiritual journeys, Washington's formation included a series of ups and downs -- three steps forward and two back.

Perhaps it is not his perfection, but on the contrary, his imperfection and struggle that are his most profound gift to us.

His earnest struggles and his lifelong process of transformation ultimately led him to a deep sense of hope; an unshakeable trust in God's mysterious ways.

Washington developed a profound understanding of the Communion Cup, with multiple allusions to both *"the cup of suffering"* and *"the cup of blessing."* Ultimately, he learned that the struggle and the perseverance in prayer would lead to an abiding joy he frequently called *"Happiness."*

Over time, Washington learned to embrace both joys and sorrows, as he made the commitment to inner work that led to spiritual growth and integrity.

Steeped in an Anglican Christian, albeit privately expressed, faith, Washington gradually seemed to recognize that his own life, and even the life of the new nation, followed the pattern of Christ's suffering and resurrection. He learned to give thanks for God's saving hand in all of life, in both good times and bad.

Grounded in prayer and honest self-reflection, Washington was transformed over the span of a lifetime. Ultimately, his humility and integrity led him to great power -- and to his humble, unheard-of conviction to let go of that power.

Over time, Washington perceived that life's challenges and losses that stretch us and change us are all part of what he called *"the inscrutable ways of Providence."*

Ultimately, he decided God's ways were mysterious but trustworthy. In the midst of all the trials Washington suffered personally and professionally, he grew to possess an unshakeable vision that Providence would ultimately birth the new nation and bless it with *"Happiness."*

What was the "secret" to Washington's belief in Providence's *"inscrutable ways,"* especially in the face of immense suffering? What was the source of his vision for a blessed and happy nation? And how did he grow into the mature faith that transformed him into an exemplar for the ages?

First and foremost, George Washington discovered meaning, purpose and joy by experiencing life through a Christian lens. He was raised in the ethos of a moderate, balanced, and broad-minded Anglican (Church of England) theology.

Formed in the latitudinarian, or broad, Anglican theology of the 18th century, he frequently communicated a wide vision for other expressions of faith. His hope was firmly rooted in a universally loving and active God. He personally continued to attend church, read scripture, and pray all his life. And he sought to integrate his prayer with action.

Washington also strongly encouraged others – family, soldiers, and later an entire nation – to practice the spiritual discipline of prayer and gratitude to God, according to their own faith traditions. Washington established America's national Thanksgiving Day observance. And he was a tireless champion of the Freedom of Religion.

Prolific biographer Douglas Southall Freeman describes an older George Washington as having identified *"religion and morality as the two great pillars of Human Happiness."*[5]

In his prolific writings, Washington uses the word "happy," often interchangeably with "joy." Derivatives of this word are found more than 1,800 times in George Washington's documented letters, maxims, and diaries.[6]

What led Washington through lifelong struggles and suffering toward this deep sense of trust and joy in God's providence and blessing?

This book navigates Washington's lifelong process of spiritual formation and his path to integrity and joy. It illustrates how his human struggles and spiritual journey were not so very different from our own. And it demonstrates how his early formation was nurtured in a significant way at Pohick Church.

2

Childhood Loss: A Mother's Praying Influence

According to the Washington family Bible, George was born in February of 1732 and baptized into the Christian faith two months later, on April 5. The momentous event took place in the small Anglican church near his parents' farm in Westmoreland County, Virginia.

Washington was raised by parents who were Anglican, or Church of England. The Anglican Church was the established church in the Pre-Revolutionary War colonies, led by England's monarch.

Washington's great-great grandfather, the Rev. Lawrence Washington, had been an Anglican priest in England. Throughout his lifetime, George remained a member of that denomination, which became the Protestant American Episcopal Church after the Revolution.

George's father Augustine Washington, a planter and businessman, married a second wife Mary Ball after his first wife died. The family spent time both at the Westmoreland County farm and at Mount Vernon.

From 1735-1737, Augustine was a vestryman of Truro Parish at Pohick Church, which was about six miles from Mount Vernon, and roughly the same distance to George Mason's Gunston Hall.

The first Pohick Church was a wooden structure constructed in 1732 on Old Colchester Road, a mile from the current Pohick Church built in 1774. Pohick Church was the seat of Truro Parish.

In those days, a parish consisted of a large geographical area with several churches, called a "parish." Pohick Church was the seat of Truro Parish. Its "vestry" was a board of elders elected as spiritual models and temporal leaders managing the business of the parish. It was the vestry's responsibility to call a priest to be Rector. Washington's father, Augustine, was a member of the vestry that called Pohick's first Rector, The Rev. Charles Green.[7]

Washington's mother Mary Ball Washington was known for her contemplative spirituality. She insisted that her children both pray and read scripture daily. Other spiritual practices of the day included teaching Anglican children to read with their Bible as their primer. Parents drilled children in the Anglican catechism, steeped in Jesus Christ. They stocked their households with books of sermons and other religious treatises. [8]

Anglican Clergy helped ground young Washington in the Christian precepts of the Catechism, which included statements like, "*I heartily thank our heavenly Father, that he hath called me to this state of salvation, through Jesus Christ our Savior. And I pray unto God to give me his grace, that I may continue in the same unto my life's end.*"

The Catechism also included the Apostle's Creed, the Ten Commandments, a statement on the Trinity, the Lord's Prayer, and instruction on the Sacraments, including Baptism and Holy Communion.

Mary Ball also often gathered her children around her and read aloud from Matthew Hale's 1685 edition of *Contemplations Moral and Divine.* Signed by Mary Ball Washington, that book now resides in Mount Vernon's Fred W. Smith Presidential Library of George Washington. A collection of Biblical principles, *Contemplations* inspired several maxims George Washington would later repeat as an adult. Hale was known for being broad-minded and inclusive regarding religious matters.

Other books in the family library may have influenced young Washington's spiritual formation. One was Thomas Comer's 1712 *Short Discourses upon the Whole Book of Common Prayer: Designed to Inform the Judgement and Excite the Devotion of Such as Daily Use the Same.* This book was signed by both his parents and later by George himself, when he was 13 years old. [9]

Another was a book of eight sermons by The Rev. Offspring Blackhall, dating from 1717: *The Sufficiency of a Standing Revelation in General and of the Scripture Revelation in Particular, Preached in the Cathedral Church of St. Paul.*" About 8 years old at the time, young Washington signed his name on this book. The Washingtons' well-read book of sermons was based on lectures Blackhall gave that proposed a latitudinarian world view, which one scholar said:

> *"...sought to articulate an Anglican theology sufficiently broad and inclusive, to comprehend many of the dissenters, and were prepared to make concessions on points of doctrine and practice to achieve that end. They were keen to emphasize, with John Locke, the reasonableness of Christianity, and to explain away its mysteries and seeming paradoxes. They were prepared to argue against atheists and deists on their own terms and to defend the credibility of the Christian experience in terms of ordinary human reason, experience and testimony."* [10]

The collecting, reading and signing of spiritual books and sermons was a discipline that Washington would continue to practice throughout his lifetime. His boyhood practices of prayer, worship, and reading scripture and other spiritual books and sermons, helped form his sense of God's revelation through human experience and through nature.

At his parents' knees, Washington was formed in the Christian faith, through the Anglican tradition. He was formed in the broad, inclusive Anglican ethos that emphasized reason and moderation, profoundly influencing his evolving leadership.

Also influencing the formation of George's moral character, were some books that were not written by Anglican clergy but that dealt with morality and civility. Sometime before his 16th birthday, George copied a list of 110 *Rules of Civility and Decent Behavior in Company and in Conversation*. Four of these rules dealing with God, religion and scripture. In a journal he kept as a teenager, Washington wrote, *"If you can't find it in Ezekiel, look for it in Israel."* [11]

Throughout his life, Washington's thinking and writing indicate that he had internalized several Biblical principles as a child. Later, he would often include Biblical phrases in his correspondence.

For instance, in his famous Circular Letter to the States at the end of the American Revolution, Washington almost directly quoted an Old Testament prophet, praying that God would:

> *"most graciously be pleased to dispose us all to do Justice, and to love mercy."*

In the same prayer, Washington alludes to Jesus Christ as he concludes:

> *"...and to demean ourselves of that charity, humility, and pacific temper which were the characteristics of the Divine Author of our blessed religion."*[12]

As he grew spiritually, Washington also demonstrated a deep appreciation of the mystery of the Sacraments that he encountered in childhood. Perhaps he began to internalize the meaning of Christ's Paschal Mystery of suffering, death and resurrection as he experienced that mystery in his own life.

His own father died an untimely death, and he also grieved the early death of his beloved half-brother Laurence. Yet through that valley of the shadow of death, Washington also experienced the dawning of new hope, meaning and purpose.

Even as a child, Washington developed a profound spiritual appreciation for the Communion Cup. Over time, Washington would frequently refer to the *"cup of suffering"* or *"cup of sorrows"* when writing or speaking about serious challenges and loss. When alluding to life's sufferings and joys, he made references to the symbolism of the Eucharistic cup at least 80 times.[13]

The phrases *"cup of suffering," "cup of sorrows" and "cup of blessings*" refer to the Communion Cup. Also called a "chalice,' the Cup was used regularly by Anglicans in Holy Communion.

The Washington family donated to Pohick Church a silver chalice stamped "1737." Pohick's Washington family chalice now resides in the Mount Vernon Museum. The Washington family drank from that cup when they participated in Communion. George Washington would have comprehended its spiritual meaning.

Abundant in imagery and meaning, the phrase *"Drinking the Cup"* alludes to sharing in Christ's own suffering and death that lead to resurrection joy. In later years, he frequently used this Eucharistic language.

Washington seemed to possess a deeply incarnational, Christian sense of being changed into Christ's likeness by drinking from the cup, or participating in Christ's suffering, death and resurrection.

Throughout his childhood, George was formed in Judeo-Christian Biblical principles, in the Anglican ethos of toleration and moderation, in sacramental theology, and in morality and civility.

Though not expressing it by name, Washington lived into the lifelong process of *theosis,* whereby one integrates prayer and action, is gradually transformed, and participates in the divine.

All of these experiences, practices and values would influence Washington's evolving perseverance, trust, humility, and dependence on God.

As Washington grew into adulthood, and wrestled with the questions most humans ask, his inner work of spiritual formation would spark his passion for unity, freedoms, the inclusivity of all religions, and his insistence on prayer and integrity.

3

Young Adulthood: Maturing through a Wilderness Journey

"Then Jesus was led by the Spirit into the wilderness to be tempted by the devil. After fasting for 40 days and forty nights, he was hungry." -- Matthew 4:1-11

God has a way of catching the attention of idealistic young adults by transforming and maturing them in the midst of wilderness journeys. In the process, they tend to affirm their identity and glimpse the meaning and purpose of their lives.

The journey motif runs through secular stories of young people's odysseys, as well as several stories in both Hebrew and Christian Scriptures.

For instance, it was into the wilderness that God led Moses and his people. It was in the wilderness that God met with Elijah. And in the wilderness, God spoke to John the Baptist. The wilderness was also where the Spirit lead Jesus after his baptism.

Wilderness wanderings are often characterized by solitude, isolation, challenges, temptations, and trials. Often, unbridled optimism and rose-colored glasses characterize youngsters on the front end of a wilderness trek. Trials and failures generally follow. Transformation occurs on the back end. Ultimately, wilderness journeys lead to a dawning awareness of a divine presence, a deepening reliance on God, and a clarified sense of identity, meaning and purpose.

In Jesus' wilderness experience, he faces the temptations of power, control, and self-reliance. In the wilderness he discovers his true identity as the Son of God. In a vast desert marked by ravenous beasts, cold hungry nights, and demonic temptations, Jesus discovers God's presence, and his reliance upon God's love, grace, and power.

As a young man, Washington would have been familiar with Jesus' wilderness experience, his coming of age, and affirmation of his identity and purpose – and of course, Jesus' death and resurrection. He had read or heard those Scriptures about Christ all his life, both by his mother's side and in Anglican worship and study.

Washington explicitly mentions Jesus Christ by name in a speech to the Delaware Nation during his own wilderness journey:

"You do well to wish to learn our arts and ways of life, and above all, the religion of Jesus Christ. These will make you a greater and happier people than you are."

Just as Jesus encountered God's presence and providence in the wilderness, it was in the wilderness of the French and Indian War

that young Washington encountered trials, tribulations, failures –
and *"Providence."* At 22 years old, in the vast forests of Ohio, George
first mentions his dawning reliance on *Providence,* a term many of
his contemporaries used as synonym for God.

Washington's life was in danger a couple of times as a Colonel in
that war. He wrote to his friend and biographer David Humphreys
of an event in which he was caught between friendly fire, and was
spared.

Later he experienced another close brush with death. General
Braddock lead Washington and other American and British soldiers to Fort Duquesne. The natives and French ambushed the
unsuspecting soldiers. Washington, who had warned the general of
potential ambush, was the only officer not wounded or killed.

David Barton, author of *The Bulletproof George Washington,"*
wrote:

> *"I expected every moment to see him fall. Nothing but the super-
> intending care of Providence could have saved him."*

After this battle, Washington wrote a somewhat humorous yet
faith-filled letter to his brother, John Augustine Washington, refer-
ring to *"the miraculous care of Providence."* He wrote these words:

> *"Dear Jack: As I have heard since my arrival at this place, a
> circumstantial account of my death and dying speech, I take this
> early opportunity of contradicting both, and of assuring you that
> I now exist and appear in the land of the living by the miraculous
> care of Providence..."[14]*

Later, in hindsight of similar experiences, Washington rewrote the end of this account with these words:

"But by the All-Powerful Dispensations of Providence, I have been protected beyond all human probability or expectations; for I had four bullets through my coat, and two horses shot under me, yet escaped unhurt, although death was leveling companions on every side of me!" [15]

From young adulthood, Washington articulated that he believed he was protected by Providence. Perhaps his wilderness journey helped shape his growing sense of identity, destiny and purpose.

Yet, as a young man with limited life experience, Washington also appeared to possess a youthful and not always realistic optimism, which might best be described as "wearing rose-colored glasses."

Although he was evolving into the leader he would one day become, he still clung to a somewhat blind trust in God's providential care. His trust was based on experiencing positive circumstances and outcomes. As a young adult, Washington seemed naively convinced that the "proof" of Providential care was that his life was spared.

Over the next several decades, Washington's youthful optimism would mature. His faith would be tested, tried, and ultimately, deepened into a more realistic trust in God – whatever the circumstances.

Evolving over a lifetime, Washington would one day articulate that humanity experiences inexplicable suffering and death. He would gradually come to believe that God cannot be explained or completely understood – yet God is present in the midst of all of life, ultimately transforming suffering and despair into joy and hope.

4

Incarnational Adulthood: Integrity and Leadership Formed at Pohick

"Abide in my Word, and my Word will abide in you..." and *"I have told you these things that my joy may be in you, and that your joy may be complete."* -- Jesus in John 15: 4 & 15

At the age of 29, as a full-fledged adult following in the footsteps of his father Augustine, Washington was elected vestryman of Pohick Church in 1761. This is a fact that is recorded in the church's original Vestry Minutes from that era.

Thanks to the return of original Vestry Minutes found in a former parishioner's attic, Pohick Church owns the hand-written records of vestry meetings spanning the years 1732 to 1785. Pohick is grateful that those original minutes are now on loan and preserved in the George Washington Presidential Library at Mount Vernon. [16]

Based on several sources – from Pohick's Vestry Minutes, from an understanding of Anglican (Church of England) theology and ethos, and from Washington's own correspondence - one can perceive the arc of Washington's spiritual growth during the next phase of his life.

This chapter explores the years during which Washington married Martha Washington and focused on updating and expanding Mount Vernon. It was during this era that he became an established Church of England (Anglican) leader at Pohick, and a community leader, as well.

Washington's social status and spiritual journey were enhanced when he met and married a young, wealthy widow Martha Washington, who was also a devout Anglican. With the help of Martha's inheritance, Washington built up Mount Vernon. Meanwhile, influenced by Martha's gentle insistence on prayer and worship, Washington continued to grow in his spiritual life.

Worshiping primarily at Pohick Church up until the Revolutionary War years, Washington was formed in a broad-minded, inclusive, latitudinarian ethos of Anglican spirituality.

As part of the established Church of England, Pohick embraced a *"via media,"* the ethos of the "middle way," that surely made an impact on Washington.

A term coined by early English reformation theologian Richard Hooker, the *"via media"* describes the *"both/and"* ethos of the Anglican faith. The *via media* is about being *both* Protestant *and* Catholic, and embracing *both* Word *and* sacrament, *both* prayer *and* action.

The very essence of being Anglican is to embrace tolerance, practice moderation, employ reason, and hold opposing views in tension. Later, these qualities and characteristics would be widely recognized and respected in Washington.

The key to Anglican spirituality lies in the Incarnation of Jesus Christ, who is *both* human *and* divine. This informs the Anglican emphasis on the lifelong process of *theosis*: imitating and embodying Christ's love, and gradually growing, transforming, and becoming one with Christ.

Washington sought to imitate and embody Christ in his own life, and frequently entreated others to do the same. Years later, in his classic circular letter to the states, he would implicitly refer to Christ as *"the divine author of our faith."* He also insisted that, only by imitating the divine author, could America hope to be *"happy,"* or find joy.

In that letter, Washington prayed that:

> *"God would most graciously be pleased to dispose us all, to do Justice, to love mercy, and to demean ourselves with that charity, humility and pacific temper of mind, which were the characteristics of the Divine Author of our Blessed Religion (Jesus Christ), and without an humble imitation of whose example in these things, we can never hope to be a Happy Nation."*

Thus, without explicitly saying the name, Washington was affirming that Jesus Christ was loving, humble, peace loving, and worthy of imitation.[17]

Indeed, the imitation of Christ and integrity of prayer and action were hallmarks of Washington's faith. Integrity of character was key. Martha's granddaughter Nellie Parke Custis would illustrate this in her testimony of Washington's Christian faith:

"He was a silent, thoughtful man. He spoke little generally, never of himself... After forty years of devoted affection and uninterrupted happiness, (Martha) surrendered (George) without a murmur into the arms of his Savior and his God, with the assured hope of eternal felicity. Is it necessary that anyone should certify, 'George Washington avowed himself to me a believer in Christianity?' As well we may question his patriotism, his heroic, disinterested devotion to his country. His mottoes were 'Deeds, not words,' and 'For God and my country.'" [18]

In other words, Nellie was saying that her step-grandfather's brand of Christianity, although mostly quiet and private, was incarnational – embodied, with integrity. If ever there were a description of classic Anglican incarnational spirituality as it is meant to be lived, Nellie's description captures it perfectly.

Furthermore, the essence of Anglican theology is to remain unified in the essentials, with the freedom to disagree in the non-essentials. Old friends George Washington and George Mason, both Pohickians, agreed on the essentials, but occasionally disagreed about the non-essentials.

For instance, when the original, wooden Pohick church began to deteriorate, Pohick's Vestry Minutes record that Washington and Mason had a "warm discussion" about the future location of the "new" Pohick Church.

George Mason argued that the new church should be built on the site of the old church – an easy commute to his home, Gunston Hall. However, Washington was not keen on crossing Pohick Creek by horseback. Using data gleaned from surveying the nearby land, Washington created a map illustrating the proximity of his and other parishioners' homes to another location, about a mile away.

Washington won that skirmish with Mason. Importantly, throughout that disagreement and others – some involving the development of the Constitution of the United States - the two remained in Communion and partook of the Eucharist shoulder-to-shoulder at Pohick's communion rail. They maintained a mutual civility and lived into their baptismal vow of dignity and respect, even when hotly debating an issue.

Biographer Douglas Freedman reported that on Sunday, July 17, 1774, the two Georges met after attending services at Pohick Church to debate the particulars of *The Fairfax Resolves*. They didn't agree on every point. They argued passionately. Yet they did so civilly, and with mutual respect.

The Fairfax Resolves were written 250 years ago, the same year the doors of the new Pohick Church were opened, in 1774. Those Resolves later evolved into the Virginia Resolves, then the Bill of Rights. The Virginia documents influenced America's Bill of Rights, enumerating personal freedoms and advocating the pursuit of happiness.

According to a plaque erected in the Pohick Courtyard in 2024, the Fairfax Resolves were signed by 25 Virginians – 13 of whom were Pohickians. The plaque recognizes the impact of the Resolves and lists those affiliated with Pohick Church:

> *"The Rev. Lee Massey, Rector 1767-1777*

> *Charles Broadwater, Martin Cockburn, Henry Gunnell, George Mason, Edward Payne, William Payne, Thomas Pollard, George Washington and John West"*

> *(as well as others investing in Pohick or interred at Pohick.)*

The Anglican latitudinarian, "broad-church" ethos of the day surely shaped Washington's passion for religious tolerance (freedom of religion). His weekly immersion in the Gospel shaped his views on unity, civility, and liberty in pursuit of happiness.

Often, Washington passionately made his arguments with countless Biblical Old Testament and New Testament references. He alluded to Old Testament prophets as he sought justice. He made countless pleas to his troops and later his nation, for ongoing prayer and thanksgiving to *the divine author of our faith* (Jesus).

Yet Washington's Christian beliefs and actions have come into question by some of his biographers. There is debate about whether Washington was a "true Christian."

Skeptics point to several "qualifiers." Christian qualifiers are based on whether the one making the judgment is Evangelical, Catholic, or somewhere in-between. The Anglican faith, meant to be somewhere in-between, was and is unequivocally Christian, professing a Trinitiarian God and the belief in Jesus' incarnation, suffering, death and resurrection. Washington understood himself as an Anglican Christian.

Others question whether Washington actually participated in Communion – and how regularly. In particular, some critics cite his "infrequent" reception of Communion as evidence he was not Christian. Others claim Washington "never took communion" – and therefore "may not have been truly Christian."

Below are arguments to the contrary – all of which pertain to Washington's spiritual apprehension of the Eucharist (Holy Communion): (1) Washington's frequency of receiving Communion was in line with colonial habits, usually offered only four or fewer times a year; (2) the Washington family donated and used a silver chalice; (3) Washington likely struggled personally with conscience in a certain period of his life; and (4) Washington's correspondence frequently includes Eucharistic language and metaphor.

First, Communion was only offered four times a year in those days, and it was possible to miss some of those occasions. On most Sundays when Communion was not offered, congregants would pray the Daily Office, such as Morning Prayer. This service included prayers, Scripture readings, and homilies – but no Communion. Prior to the war, barring sickness or a conflicting schedule, Washington's family reported that he partook of the Eucharist as regularly as the church celebrated it.

Second, in 1734, two years after George was born, the Washington family ordered, donated, and doubtless drank from, a silver chalice (cup) given to Pohick Church. That chalice now resides on loan from Pohick in the Mount Vernon Museum, next to the model exhibit of Pohick Church. The underside of the chalice is stamped with the Washington name. To this day, the Rector of Pohick Church annually lifts that same Washington family chalice while celebrating the Eucharist on Mount Vernon's piazza. (This special Communion service takes place during the annual meeting of the Mount Vernon Ladies Association.)

Third, the accounts of Washington leaving services "before communion" happened only after the Revolutionary War. A very likely explanation for his alleged avoidance of Communion at that point was his ongoing quest for integrity. Why did he struggle with integrity with regard to Communion?

Washington was probably conflicted about being "in communion" with the Church of England. After all, the colonies had broken with England's monarch, who was also the head of the Church of England. During the Revolution, Washington also parted ways with several clergy who remained loyal to the Crown. He likely felt hypocritical about partaking in Communion with adherents to the Crown.

Also, with all the death and destruction Washington witnessed during the war, he surely wrestled daily with difficult moral decisions he was called to make as Commander in Chief. Washington's struggle with the integrity of Communion under these trying circumstances made him more, not less, a true Christian! The inner struggle actually made him more human!

Fourth, throughout his life and particularly during and after the Revolution, Washington frequently employed Eucharistic language in his correspondence. He regularly used phrases like, *"the Cup of Suffering"* and *"the Cup of Blessing,"* among several other clear references to the Communion Cup. (These will be further explored in a later chapter.) Washington deeply intuited and embraced the metaphorical and spiritual meaning of the Eucharist.

Pohick's Vestry Minutes also indicate that Washington purchased a large, turkey leather-bound liturgical 1662 Book of Common Prayer for use in corporate worship. He was tasked by the vestry to order this book from the Church of England.

One of the great delights about that corporate Book of Common Prayer (still in Pohick's possession) is that it contains a prayer for England's Monarch that was carefully and completely scratched through, with ink, probably by clergy.

Apparently, praying for one's enemies was not a practice that patriotic Pohickians wholeheartedly embraced!

Washington also ordered a beautiful reredos for Pohick Church. Rising up behind the altar, the reredos is a backdrop emblazoned with the 10 commandments and prayers proclaiming a Trinitarian faith and belief in Jesus' death and resurrection. Although the original reredos was later destroyed by an encampment of Union soldiers, the design and language of the current, restored reredos are identical to the original.

Washington possessed a deep appreciation for the "beauty of holiness." The Vestry Minutes report that he personally ordered the gold gilt lettering for the prayers and commandments on the reredos. He also ordered a lovely marble baptismal font to be shipped from England.

Washington and his family attended services at Pohick regularly. Several eyewitnesses corroborate this fact. His own diaries record days when he *"attended Pohick Church."*

Visitors frequently mentioned that Washington would invite them to attend church with him. One scholar who closely examined Washington's diaries reported that he attended church an average of once a month – a typical attendance pattern for his contemporaries.

In his correspondence he often spoke fondly of Christmas, writing to friends and family repeated messages like:

> *"I hope that the next Christmas will prove happier than the present..." or "I may on these accounts venture to hope that you will spend a happy and merry Christmas."*

In particular, he mentions Christmas at Pohick Church. His journal entry for December 25, 1770, reads: *"Went to Pohick Church and returned for dinner."*

When Washington attended Pohick, his devoted conduct apparently influenced and inspired other congregants. The Rev. Lee Massey, Rector of Pohick Church during Washington's vestry years, recalled his attendance as exemplary. Massey, who was later buried under Pohick's pulpit, described Washington's presence like this:

> *"I never knew so constant an attendant at church as Washington. His behavior in the House of God was ever so reverential that*

it produced the happiest effects on my congregation, and greatly assisted me in my pulpit labours." [19]

[Author's note: As 16th Rector of Pohick, I humbly "pinched myself" when preaching and gazing at parishioners from that same raised pulpit! Looking at the upturned faces of beloved parishioners, one can easily imagine the rapt faces of George and Martha Washington and other colonial families. Current-day Pohickians still embody that reverence, *"producing the happiest effects,"* and *"assisting in pulpit labours!"*]

Martha Washington's personal Book of Common Prayer that she carried to church still resides in the inner sanctum of the Washington Presidential Library. She was known to be a devout Christian and avid church goer who surely influenced her husband's faith. The Washingtons spent hours reading and discussing Scripture, as well as sermons they collected over the years.

Finally, lest readers harbor lingering doubts as to Washington's formation as a Christian, his precious step-granddaughter, Nellie Custis, once described his spiritual habits of daily prayer and the integrity of his actions:

"It was his custom to retire to his library at nine or ten o'clock, where he remained about an hour before he returned to his chamber. He always rose before the sun, and remained in his library until called to breakfast. I never witnessed his private devotions; I never inquired about them, I should have thought it the greatest heresy to doubt his firm belief in Christianity. His life, his writings, prove that he was a Christian. He was not one of those who

act or pray, 'that they might be seen of men.' He communed with his God in secret." [20]

Supporting Nelly's observations about Washington's incarnational spirituality – his prayer embodied in action -- are several other eyewitnesses:

His nephew Major George Lewis, who served as Washington's bodyguard in the Revolution, overheard Washington's early morning prayers when he arrived to deliver new dispatches to his room. Lewis said he retired to another part of the house until the morning devotions had been completed. He was also known for returning to prayer every night before retiring to bed.

Witnesses to the death of Martha Parke Custis reported that Washington knelt by her bed and *"solemnly recited the prayers for the dying* (from the 1662 Anglican Book of Common Prayer) – *while tears rolled down his cheeks, and his voice was often broken by sobs."* [21]

According to a Presbyterian minister's recollection, at meals Washington generally stood and said grace, unless there was a clergyman present who could be asked to say prayers before and after the meal. [22]

As a maturing adult who regularly attended and served at Pohick Church, Washington grew into his gifts as a spiritual and temporal leader. At Pohick and elsewhere, Washington quietly and intentionally lived into the incarnational spirituality of abiding in Christ.

For Washington, the spiritual disciplines of praying and studying God's Word were non-negotiables. So was integrity of life. Yet his process of spiritual formation spanned a lifetime. He did not "arrive" overnight.

Far from perfect, Washington prayerfully grew over time. Beginning as a young leader at Pohick Church and continuing throughout his life, Washington consciously struggled to integrate his spiritual practices and beliefs with his actions. Furthermore, he encouraged others to do the same.

Ultimately, his incarnational spirituality would lead Washington to fully embrace the joy, the *"cup of blessing,"* the *"happiness,"* as he so frequently described it, that is the fruit of integrity.

Washington's greatest gift to future generations was not spiritual or moral perfection. On the contrary, Washington's very imperfection – his human suffering, his humble and honest self-reflection, and his willingness to evolve through prayer and integrity of action -- were surely among his greatest contributions.

5

A General's Pain: The Cup of Suffering

"Father, if you are willing, take this cup from me…"
-- Jesus in the Garden of Gethsemane (Luke 22:42)

" We are afflicted in every way, but not crushed; perplexed, but not driven to despair; persecuted but not forsaken; struck down but not destroyed."
-- St. Paul in his Second Letter to the Corinthians (2 Cor 4:8-9)

"I want to know Christ and the power of his resurrection and the sharing of his sufferings by becoming like him in his death…experience Christ's suffering and death, and so, somehow attain to his resurrection from the dead."
-- St. Paul in his Letter to the Philippians (Phil 3:10)

Although Washington ultimately embraced the Communion *"cup of blessing,"* it was not without a significant struggle with the *"cup of suffering."* As Christians are fond of saying, one cannot fully appreciate Easter without experiencing the transformative effects of Good Friday.

Washington experienced suffering at many junctures in his life, beginning perhaps with the untimely death of his father. Over time, he experienced the losses of several beloved family members and friends -- as well as fellow soldiers.

General Washington's firsthand knowledge of the suffering of his soldiers during the Revolutionary War uniquely challenged and deeply transformed his spiritual life. From accounts of his prayers as well as his journals, it is clear that during this phase of his life, Washington wrestled with the classic Christian problem of suffering and evil.

Remaining in proximity with his soldiers, Washington encountered suffering in ways that most humans will never experience. Along the way, his relationship with God became less contingent on his glib confidence and blind optimism in a favorable outcome (as in his younger days in the French and Indian War) -- and more based on realistic trust in God's *"inscrutable ways"* in spite of the outcome.

Based on Washington's diary entries and the observation of soldiers and colleagues, one can observe Washington's spiritual evolution during this excruciatingly painful time.

In the diary he kept at Valley Forge, General Washington commented on the desolate condition of his men and the discouraging progress of the war. He offered a spiritual context for their struggles:

"Ours is a kind of struggle designed, I dare say, by Providence, to try the patience and fortitude and virtue of men. None, therefore, who is engaged in it, will suffer himself, I trust, to sink under difficulties, or to be discouraged by hardships. If he cannot do as he wishes, he must do what he can." [23]

At this point in his life, Washington had come to believe that God sometimes brings (or allows) suffering as a way of testing character. From the same passage, author Stephen Vicchio maintains that Washington was a believer in *divine plan theory* when it came to explaining the problem of suffering and evil.

In a letter, Washington said:

"I will not lament or repine any at any act of Providence, because I am in a great measure a convert to Mr. Pope's opinion that 'whatever is, is right.' [24]

Washington is alluding to Alexander Pope's poem, *"An Essay on Man"* Pope was a follower of German philosopher GW Leibniz's *divine plan theory.* Washington seems to embrace that theory. Several times, Washington regularly responds to the problem of evil and suffering by proclaiming that *"all is in the hands of a Good Providence— "* which was an 18th century catchphrase for the divine plan, according to Vicchio.

Divine plan theory is a more forward-looking response to the problem of suffering and evil, as opposed to some of the backward-looking theories. Looking backward to explain evil and suffering, one might point to a "cause" – like original sin, demonic forces, or the free will defense.

In contrast, a more forward-looking response to evil and suffering, the divine plan theory suggests that something may appear to be an example of evil or suffering in the short run. In the long run, however, one will eventually see that everything works out for the good. In contemporary Christianity, those who assent to this philosophical view might say, "God has his own purposes."

Among the major religions of the world, most fall somewhere on a continuum of theories about evil and suffering. Christianity, Judaism and Islam are religions of paradox, in the middle. They believe everything comes from God, and God is all good – yet on the other hand, these religions of paradox also believe in the existence of the demonic.

Washington was no stranger to suffering. His own father died young, as did his beloved half-brother Lawrence and later his step-niece Patsy. Washington contracted smallpox himself, the disease that killed Lawrence, and scarred his own face for life.

Then there was the winter of 1777-78 at Valley Forge, the low point of the Revolutionary War which tried Washington's faith to the point of near despair.

Even with his firsthand knowledge of the suffering of his men, Washington seemed to have coped with that suffering with patience, perseverance, and courage. In his diary at Valley Forge in the winter of 1777, Washington gave the struggles a theological context of the divine plan theory that leaves room for this paradox and offers a practice response:

"Ours is a struggle designed, I dare say, by Providence, to try the patience and fortitude and virtue of men. None, therefore, who is engaged in it, will suffer himself, I trust, to sink under difficulties

or be discouraged by hardships. If he cannot do what he wishes, he must do what he can." [25]

Here the general demonstrates belief in several responses to the problem of evil in Christianity, Judaism and Islam. One of these is the moral qualities perspective: he was saying his soldiers developed patience and fortitude when God allowed suffering to come to them. "Discouraged by hardships" alludes to the test perspective, in that God sometimes allows evil and suffering as a way of "testing" and molding them. [26]

Washington ultimately responded to suffering in his own life and in those around him with the theological response that God's ways are mysterious. This lines up with his favorite description of God's ways: *"inscrutable."*

As he matured, Washington came to understand that there is also an element of unexplainable mystery in the problem of evil and suffering. In his messages of comfort to those experiencing great loss, Washington frequently used these phrases, *'the inscrutable ways of Providence,"* and the *"unsearchable ways of Providence."*

Mary Thompson sums up Washington's understanding of Providence with respect to the problem of suffering and evil when she writes:

> *"Washington appears to have believed that, while God/Providence directed the course of events on earth, human beings could not always understand why certain things occurred and simply had to turn to their reasoning powers and their religious beliefs to make sense of it all, and in the end, come to the acceptance of God's will."* [27]

When Washington was writing or speaking about serious challenges and losses, he would frequently use Eucharistic language. In fact, he referred to the *"cup of suffering" or the "cup of sorrows,"* using those phrases more than 80 times in his vast correspondence and journals. [28]

The "cup of suffering" or "cup of sorrows" are metaphors for the cup of Christ's blood, or the Eucharistic (Communion) Cup. Also called a "chalice," the cup was used regularly by Anglicans in Holy Communion. As mentioned earlier, the Washington family donated a silver chalice, stamped "1737," to Pohick Church. The family surely drank from that cup when they participated in Communion.

In classic catholic theology, partaking in the Communion Cup means one is participating in the mystery of the life, death and resurrection of Jesus Christ. Thus, when Washington used Communion Cup imagery, he was not only being profoundly Christian; he was also expressing a deep belief that suffering can be redemptive and lead to new and transformed life, integrity, and joy (*"Happiness."*)

Rife with imagery and meaning, the phrase *"drinking the cup"* ultimately alludes to *theosis.* This is a theological term meaning the process of conversion that involves participating in Christ's sufferings and being changed into Christ's own likeness.

Washington seemed to believe that in communing with Providence – whether by prayer or by actually partaking in Communion -- one was changed, and was expected to behave as if united in Spirit with Christ.

He uses the Biblical metaphor of the Communion Cup in several practical contexts and in writings throughout his life, including:

- *"The Bitter Cup."* Evoking the sharing of Jesus' suffering and contemplation of pending death, when he was in the Garden of Gethsemane, Washington often used this phrase to comment on the horrific suffering of prisoners of war. For instance, he wrote:

"...impeding the progress both of drafting and recruiting, by dejecting the courage of the soldiery from an apprehension of the horrors of captivity, and finally by reducing those whose lot is to drink the bitter cup, to a despair..."

- *"The Cup of Reconciliation."* Later, as President of the United States, he wrote on July 13, 1778, from Mount Vernon:

  "Satisfied, therefore, that you have sincerely wished and endeavored to avert war, and exhausted to the last drop, the cup of reconciliation..."

- *"The Cup of Blessing"* (using the synonym, Cup of *"Beneficence"*). In another variation of the phrase, Washington later alluded to the spirit of the Communion Cup in his most public letter, the Circular Letter written to the governors of the States, at the end of the war, in 1783:

  "That as the all-wise dispenser of human blessings has favored no nation of the earth with more abundant and substantial means of happiness than United America that we may not be so ungrateful to our Creator; so wanting to ourselves; and so regardless of posterity, as to dash the Cup of Beneficence which is thus bountifully offered to our acceptance."[29]

Importantly, Washington was not interested in theological theory or esoteric spiritual language about the Communion Cup. He was, however, very keen on putting his spiritual beliefs into daily practice. Furthermore, he modelled that integrity to his army.

Among his troops, he commanded regular prayer, and he demanded the integrity of their behavior. Several officers and enlisted reported that Washington required his soldiers to pray. Examples abound of Washington's orders to his troops for prayer and thanksgiving.

Early in the Revolution, General Washington wrote orders to his troops that they engage in regular prayer. He wrote that he *"...requires and expects of all officers and soldiers not engaged on actual duty, a punctual attendance on divine Service, to implore the blessings of heaven upon the means used for our safety and defense."* [30]

Furthermore, Washington was not requiring his soldiers to do something he did not do, as evidenced by numerous references to Washington's own regular attendance in services. He also instituted the position of army chaplain.

Washington declared many days of fasting and thanksgiving and ordered his troops to comply, praying according to their own religious tradition. One of these, declared on July 20, 1775, was mentioned in the journal of a Continental soldier:

> *"This day is devoted to a public fast throughout the united colonies, by the recommendation of Congress, to implore the divine benediction on our country; that any further shedding of blood may be averted, and that the calamities with which we are afflicted may be removed. This is the first general or Continental fast ever observed since the settlement of the colonies."* [31]

As a military leader, Washington called for prayer on a multitude of occasions at the request of the Continental Congress. In one such order he wrote in 1779, Washington used several Christian terms familiar to him, including: *"our gracious Redeemer,"* the *"light of the Gospel,"* *"the light of Christian knowledge,"* and *"the Holy Spirit."* [32]

Even though Washington often used profoundly Christian language, he always encouraged his men to pray according to their conscience. This directive to pray according to one's own beliefs reflected his compassion for the freedom of religion.

As the war dragged on, Washington regularly required his army to comply with specific orders for days of fasting and thanksgiving. One such order happened in the spring of 1778, after the French aligned themselves with the colonies to provide support.

In orders issued on May 5, Washington said with gratitude:

> *"It having pleased the Almighty Ruler of the Universe propitiously to defend the cause of the United American States, and finally by raising us up a powerful friend among the princes of the earth, to establish our liberty and independence on a lasting foundation: it becomes us to set apart a day for gratefully acknowledging the divine goodness, and celebrating the important event which we owe to his benign interposition."*

Prayer was not merely lip service for Washington. He modeled the integrity of both prayer and action. One observer of the Washington praying the above prayer was The Rev. Henry M Muhlenberg. Often described as the father of the Lutheran Church in America. Muhlenberg wrote in his journal dated May 7:

> *"I heard a fine example today, namely that His Excellency General Washington rode around among his army yesterday and admonished each and every one to fear God, to put away the wickedness*

that has set in…and to practice the Christian virtues. From all appearances, this gentleman does not belong to the so-called world of society, for he respects God's Word, believes in the atonement of Jesus Christ, and bears himself in humility and gentleness…"[33]

For Washington, the integrity of prayer lived out in moral behavior was key. This is the essence the Christian journey of death and resurrection: holding the Cup of Sorrows and being transformed by it, into a new and resurrected way of life. In particular, his commitment to integrity underscores his formation in the Anglican incarnational ethos of embodying what one believes.

Yet, this doesn't mean that Washington's journey of formation was an easy one.

Throughout his years as General of the Continental Army, and beyond, Washington struggled with the problem of suffering and evil. He experienced and wrote about what it meant to partake in Christ's *"cup of sorrows."*

Throughout those most trying times, Washington persevered in prayer, and insisted on prayer among his troops, with a broad tolerance and encouragement of all faiths. He also demanded and modeled integrity of action.

In the midst of heartbreaking loss and near despair during the Revolutionary War, Washington was again changed, learning firsthand what it means to live into Christ's paschal mystery of suffering and death.

Having moved beyond his earlier, more certain and "rose-colored" perceptions of God, Washington had come to perceive a divine design in the midst of trials and uncertainties.

Schroeder's *Maxims of Washington* records this statement from Washington in 1778:

"Ours is a kind of struggle, designed, I daresay, by Providence, to try the patience, fortitude and virtue of men." And later:

"The ways of Providence are inscrutable, and mortals must submit." [34]

The horrors of war challenged Washington to gain a less optimistic and more realistic trust in *"the inscrutable ways of Providence."* Over time, he had come to believe that God was present and working out his own divine plan – regardless of the most dire of circumstances.

6

A Planter's Struggle: The Institution of Slavery

Washington was neither a perfect person, nor was he a moral failure. One should neither idolize nor demonize him.

Washington's greatest gifts to us may have in fact been his spiritual and moral struggles, his willingness to be transformed, and his evolving trust in what he called *"the inscrutable ways of Providence."*

As mentioned earlier, *"Providence"* was a word many in his day used for God. Like the psalmist who wrote Psalm 139, Washington gradually came to see that God was unknowable, *"inscrutable."* He also came to believe we could trust God's ways, even in the face of suffering and evil.

This trust in God's ways regardless of suffering and pain was not always present in Washington's life. As mentioned earlier, when he was a youth, he lacked wisdom; his prayer life was proscribed and simple.

As a young man fighting in the French and Indian War, Washington lacked clear vision. He believed in God's presence and action only when things went well for him. When his life was spared, he naively presumed he was in God's favor.

Later, as a General of the Continental Army -- when he faced real suffering, sickness, death, and near despair -- Washington's faith deepened, and his wisdom evolved.

In the midst of immense suffering, he persevered in prayer. He ordered his troops to pray, and according to their own religious tradition. He also encouraged them to act with integrity.

During the war years, Washington showed real signs of spiritual transformation. One evidence of that the inner struggle and change of heart that continued beyond the war, was his struggle and evolving view toward the institution of slavery.

When Washington was fighting for the cause of liberty and freedom, he had often used the language, *"being freed from the shackles of England."* Watching the brave soldiers of African descent fight courageously alongside white soldiers, Washington's heart had changed. Ultimately, he integrated his army, no longer separating black from white.

Now, back home as a planter, he could hardly miss the irony of holding human beings in captivity.

During and especially after the Revolutionary War, Washington began expressing his struggle with slavery and exploring options for abolishing it.

Washington regularly corresponded with abolitionist-leaning friends, such as Marquis de Lafayette, Alexander Hamilton, and fellow Pohickian George Mason.

One Sunday in 1774, Mason and Washington left Pohick after worship and rode to Mount Vernon, where they drafted the Fairfax Resolves. The ideals of freedom and equality embodied in the Resolves influenced the American Constitution. One of its resolutions specifically addresses the abomination of owning human beings.

Owning enslaved people had always been second nature to him and to his contemporaries. He was born into a world in which slavery was a way of life – not only in the colonies, but all over the known world. This does not condone the evil of slavery, nor excuse it.

Altogether, by the time of his death in 1799, Washington and his wife Martha, owned more than 300 slaves working in clusters on five farms.[35]

Yet, between the end of the War and his Presidency, Washington continued to wrestle with the institution of slavery. Often abolitionists visited Mount Vernon, and Washington kept a collection of abolitionist pamphlets.

On May 26, 1785, two Methodist bishops who were abolitionists, Thomas Coke and Francis Asbury, visited Mount Vernon. They asked Washington to sign an anti-slavery petition.

Washington told them he shared their feelings about slavery. He told them that he had *"signified his thoughts on the subject to most of the great men of the state,"* presumably in person rather than in writing. He told them he did not see that it was proper to sign the petition, but that he would let the Virginia Assembly know his thoughts if they ever addressed the subject on the floor. Five months later, their petition was read in the legislature, and rejected. [36]

Washington's views on abolition continued to be challenged and, importantly, to evolve. Repeatedly, he reiterated his position that the best way to eliminate slavery was through legislation. He hoped the government would set up a program of gradual emancipation. His objection was no longer abolishing slavery, but landing on a method of emancipation that would not divide the newly united colonies.

In 1786, Washington told his friend Robert Morris that he hoped no one would misunderstand his opposition to certain methods as opposition to abolition. He wrote:

> *"I hope it will not be conceived from these observations, that it is my wish to hold the unhappy people who are the subject of this letter, in slavery. I can only say that there is not a man living who wishes more than I do to see a plan adopted for the abolition of it – but there is only one proper and effectual mode by which it can be accomplished, and that is by legislative authority..." [37]*

As President of the new nation, Washington came to see that the institution of slavery needed to die. His great struggle was with the method of abolishing it. He sought to do so in a measured way that did not divide the newly united colonies.

Were it to come to dividing over slavery, Washington reportedly said that he would side with the North against slavery. Near the end of his life, back at Mount Vernon under his own *"vine and fig tree,"* Washington decided to free his slaves, through his last will and testament. In doing so, Washington was unique among his contemporaries.

Twenty-first century detractors frequently demonize Washington for his ownership of slaves. Washington should neither be demonized nor placed on a pedestal. He should be admired for his inner struggles, moral grappling, and gradual evolution. Regarding the evil of slavery, Washington sought and ultimately embraced an integrity of belief and action.

This, then is the essence of Christian life – not automatic holiness, but a process of inner struggle, repentance, and transformation in the pattern of Christ's paschal mystery.

Slavery was an issue that plagued and transformed Washington over a lifetime. However, the fact remains that, when he was warden of Pohick Church, he and his fellow parishioners used slave labor to construct the church building.

As Pohick approached its 250th anniversary, research for this book inspired this author to recognize for posterity all who labored to build Pohick Church, including enslaved persons, by name. A proposal was made to research and produce a permanent plaque for the church, and the Vestry approved.

Pohick docent and historian Dick Hamly went to work researching those names. Poring over local plantation records from Fairfax County, and reading through entries in Pohick's Vestry Minutes, Hamly compiled a list of those who contributed to the construction of the 1774 building.

The list included planters like George Washington and George Mason, wardens and chairs of Pohick's building and grounds committee; Daniel French, who owned the plantation on which Pohick sits; skilled laborers and local merchants; indentured servants; and enslaved persons.

In February 2023, our Pohick Vestry erected a bronze plaque on the west wall of the church, recognizing the enslaved people who had no choice in laboring to build it. In a spirit of honest regret echoing Washington's own toward the end of his life, Pohick's plaque recognizes the issue of slavery, and thanks and immortalizes by name all who built Pohick Church, including the enslaved. The plaque reads:

"Construction of Pohick Church

Completed in 1774, this historic church was built in part with slave and indentured labor. Enslaved Americans were also employed in the fabrication of its original fixtures and furnishings. The financial support of prominent early parishioners toward the work of the church was made possible by the labor of enslaved Americans. The Clergy and People of Pohick Church recognize the vital endeavors of all who participated in the construction of this church. We are grateful for their contributions to Pohick's history and ongoing spiritual legacy.

Pohick Church Building Committee

George Washington, George Mason, William Fairfax, Daniel McCarty, Edward Payne, Peter Wegner, Martin Cockburn and Alexander Henderson

Undertakers (General Contractors):

Daniel French

George Mason

Vestry Eardens: Daniel McCarty and Thomas Coffer

Clerks at Construction Site:

Elijah Williams and Benjamin West

Suppliers Transporters, Businessmen:

George Washington, Alexander Henderson, Harry Piper, John Carylye, John Dalton, Robert Bogess, James Hardwick, Thomas

Samson, Jeremiah Cullinson, Benjamen Hatten, Daniel McCarty, Charles Cooper, Robert Adams, John Mills, Mr. Maloney, Mr. Carr, Mr Chapman, Mr. Waite, Mr. Jennifer and Mr. Hooes

Overseer:

Thomas Triplett

Stone Masons: William Copein, Hanson Harrison and Frances Coffer

Bricklayers: Appolos Cooper, Mr. Hall, Mr. Gilpin and Indentured Servant Ben Burton

Carpenters and Woodworkers:

Going Lanphier, William Bernard Sears, Zakariah Bond, and Enslaved Men Jack and Peter Shear

Pasterer and Painter: Josiah Miles

Metalsmiths: Enslaved Men George, Joe and Tom

Cook: Mary Wilson

Firewood Cutter: Enslaved Man Peter

Enslaved Africans on Site in 1772, whose particular contributions were not recorded:

Jack Goddert,, Will Goddert, Kate, Jack, Exeter, George, Viner,Lett, Sue, Philis, Betty and her Child Humphrey, Bett. Fanny, Dinah, Abraham, Isaac, Joe, Sam, Gilbert and Emanuel"

The message of the plaque's recognition is twofold: First, slavery was an evil institution, and the enslaved persons who had no choice but to labor to build Pohick are now recognized and thanked. Second: Pohick does not demonize its colonial ancestors – like George Washington, George Mason and others-- who struggled with the institution of slavery.

On the contrary, Washington can be remembered and appreciated for his human imperfections, his inner struggles, his perseverance in prayer, his humble willingness to listen to God's voice throughout his life – and ultimately for his transformation.

Washington was open to repentance and conversion of heart. He was willing to embrace the cup of suffering. He was committed to following God's call with integrity – which is the very essence of what it is to be Christian.

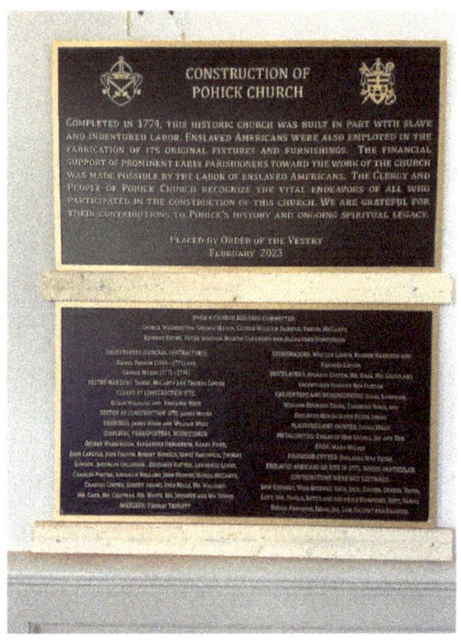

7

A President's Conversion: The Cup of Blessing

"Is not the cup of thanksgiving for which we give thanks a partici-pation in the blood of Christ? And is not the bread that we break a participation in the body of Christ?" -- 1 Corinthians 10:16

As General of the Continental Army, then as the First President of the United States, Washington's constant drumbeat of the need for prayer and thanksgiving set the tone for the new nation to remain steeped in prayer and dependent on God.

Washington's personal use of prayer and other spiritual and Biblical references only increased during his Presidency. President

Washington's vast correspondence contains more than one hundred written prayers.[38]

There is always the ready argument that Washington's secretaries and speech writers like Alexander Hamilton and Thomas Jefferson wrote the prayers for him. Yet author Peter Lillback points out that Washington himself revealed that, if prayers were not included in the drafts of his speeches or correspondence, he would regularly, personally add them.

One example is the record of a 1781 letter to Comte de Rochambeau, below, drafted by Hamilton. It includes a prayer, in brackets, which was missing in that draft, and which Washington added:

> *"I have an increase of happiness from the subsequent intelligence you do me the favor to communicate, respecting Count E'Estaings' success. This repetition of advices justifies a confidence in their truth (which I pray God may be confirmed in its greatest extent).* The words in the parentheses are added into the text by George Washington.[39]

In Washington's presidential correspondence, Eucharistic language remained prevalent. Notably, in this later phase of his life, Washington's Communion Cup references focused more on the *"cup of Blessing"* or *"cup of thanksgiving,"* than on the *"cup of suffering."*

> *"At this auspicious period, the United States came into existence as a nation, and if their citizens should not be completely free and happy, the fault will be entirely their own. Such is our situation, and such are our prospects: but notwithstanding, the cup of blessing is thus reached out to us, notwithstanding, happiness is*

ours if we have a disposition to seize the occasion and make it our own." [40]

In Washington's view, the personal and national path to the *cup of blessing* and to *happiness* demanded the country's embrace of prayer, humility, and peace – all of which he described as *"characteristics of the Divine Author of our Religion"* (Jesus Christ). In his famous Circular Letter to (the Governors) of the States, written in 1783, Washington wrote this prayer:

> *"I now make it my earnest prayer that God would have you, and the state over which you preside, in his holy protection, that he would incline the hearts of the citizens to cultivate a spirit of subordination and obedience to government, to entertain a brotherly affection and love for one another, for their fellow citizens of the United States at large and for their brethren who have served in the field, and finally that he would be most graciously pleased to dispose us all to do justice, to love mercy, and to demean ourselves with that charity, humility, and pacific temper of mind, which were the characteristics of the Divine Author of our Blessed Religion, and without an humble invitation of whose example in these things, we can never hope to be a Happy Nation."* [41]

Chief Justice of the Supreme Court John Marshall, a close personal friend who had served under Washington throughout the Revolutionary War (including at Mount Vernon) characterized faith of President Washington:

"Without making ostentation professions of religion, he (Washington) was a sincere believer in the Christian faith, and a truly devout man." [42]

There are more than 100 prayers in Washington's vast correspondence.

Washington was a lifelong Christian who worshipped in the Anglican tradition. Evidence abounds that he was an ardent, albeit quiet believer in Jesus Christ. He frequently used symbolic Eucharistic language in his writings and prayers.

Yet, one of Washington's greatest spiritual gifts to the nation was his broad tolerance and encouragement of all religious traditions.

That wide acceptance of all faith traditions may well have been influenced once again by his Anglican upbringing. In Washington's day, the Church of England's latitudinarian (broad) theology emphasized toleration of others' beliefs. Many of the Seventeenth- and Eighteenth-century Anglican clergy advocated ecclesiastical moderation, voiced broad if heavily qualified support for religious toleration, and emphasized an undogmatic, reasoned faith.

Importantly, Washington encouraged his troops and later all American citizens as well to pray according to their own belief systems. This encouragement of interfaith prayer during and after the War was based on Washington's passionate belief in human freedom – including the Freedom of Religion.

One famous example of his belief in interfaith prayer, occurred during a visit to Newport, R.I., in 1790, a year before the Bill of Rights was ratified. At that time. President Washington received a letter from Moses Seixas, warden of the Touro Synagogue, seeking assurance of religious freedom for Jews.

Washington replied, offering an unequivocal guarantee. His reply stated that the new government would *"give to bigotry no sanction, to persecution no assistance."* Below are the transcripts of both letters:

The letter from Moses Seixas to President George Washington:

To the President of the United States of America. Sir:

Permit the children of the stock of Abraham to approach you with the most cordial affection and esteem for your person and merits ~~ and to join with our fellow citizens in welcoming you to NewPort.

With pleasure we reflect on those days ~~ those days of difficulty, and danger, when the God of Israel, who delivered David from the peril of the sword, ~~ shielded Your head in the day of battle: ~~ and we rejoice to think, that the same Spirit, who rested in the Bosom of the greatly beloved Daniel enabling him to preside over the Provinces of the Babylonish Empire, rests and ever will rest, u pon you, enabling you to discharge the arduous duties of Chief Magistrate in these States.

Deprived as we heretofore have been of the invaluable rights of free Citizens, we now with a deep sense of gratitude to the Almighty disposer of all events behold a Government, erected by the Majesty of the People ~~ a Government, which to bigotry gives no sanction, to persecution no assistance ~~ but generously af- fording to all Liberty of conscience, and immunities of Citizenship: ~~ deeming every one, of whatever Nation, tongue, or language equal parts of the great governmental Machine: ~~ This so ample and extensive Federal Union whose basis is Philanthropy, Mutual confidence and Public Virtue, we cannot but acknowledge to be the work of the Great God, who ruleth in the Armies of Heaven, and among the Inhabitants of the Earth, doing whatever seemeth him good.

For all these Blessings of civil and religious liberty which we enjoy under an equal benign administration, we desire to send up our thanks to the Ancient of Days, the great preserver of Men ~~beseeching him, that the Angel who conducted our forefathers through the wilderness into the promised Land, may graciously conduct you through all the difficulties and dangers of this mortal life: ~~ And, when, like Joshua full of days and full of honour, you are gathered to your Fathers, may you be admitted into the Heavenly Paradise to partake of the water of life, and the tree of immortality.

Done and Signed by order of the Hebrew Congregation in New-Port, Rhode Island August 17th 1790. Moses Seixas, Warden

Washington's Reply to the Hebrew Congregation in Newport, Rhode Island:

Gentlemen,

Americans United for Separation of Church and State

While I receive, with much satisfaction, your Address replete with expressions of affection and esteem; I rejoice in the opportunity of assuring you, that I shall always retain a grateful remembrance of the cordial welcome I experienced in my visit to Newport, from all classes of Citizens.

Consciousness that they are succeeded by days of uncommon prosperity and security. If we have wisdom to make the best use of the advantages with which we are now favored, we cannot fail, under the just administration of a good Government, to become a great and happy people.

The Citizens of the United States of America have a right to applaud themselves for having given to mankind examples of an enlarged and liberal policy: a policy worthy of imitation. All possess alike liberty of conscience and immunities of citizenship. It is now no more that toleration is spoken of, as if it was by the indulgence of one class of people, that another enjoyed the exercise of their inherent natural rights.

For happily the Government of the United States, which gives to bigotry no sanction, to persecution no assistance requires only that they who live under its protection should demean themselves as good citizens, in giving it on all occasions their effectual support.

It would be inconsistent with the frankness of my character not to avow that I am pleased with your favor- able opinion of my Administration, and fervent wishes for my felicity. May the children of the Stock of Abraham, who dwell in this land, continue to merit and enjoy the good will of the other Inhabitants...

> *May the father of all mercies scatter light and not darkness in our paths, and make us all in our several vocations useful here, and in his own due time and way everlastingly happy.*
>
> G. Washington [43]

After Washington declined a third term out of humility and a sense of what was best for the nation, he was delighted to return home and spend his golden years as farmer, husband and step-grandfather at Mount Vernon.

By the time Washington retired from the Presidency, he had attained a level of peace and a hard-earned wisdom.

He was thrilled to be home at Mount Vernon with his family and his beloved farm. To describe his love for being home at Mount Vernon, Washington frequently alluded to yet another favorite scripture: *"Under my own vine and fig tree,"* a phrase found in three places in Hebrew scriptures, in the books of Micah, I Kings and Zechariah. The meaning of the phrase *"under my own vine and fig tree"* alluded to the independence of a peasant farmer freed from military oppression.

In his golden years, Washington regularly gave thanks for the new nation's hard-won freedoms. By this stage of his life, he also realistically recognized God's mysterious presence throughout the struggle – in the sorrows as well as the joys.

8

A Great Human's Spiritual Legacy: Trusting in Providence's Inscrutable Ways

"I AM the resurrection and the life, saith the Lord: he that believeth in me, though he were dead, yet shall he live: and whosoever liveth and believeth in me shall never die." -- John 11:25-26

Was Washington a perfect human being? No.

Was he a devout, albeit private, Anglican Christian who wrestled with his faith and attended to his inner life? Absolutely.

Perhaps Washington's greatest spiritual legacy to future generations was precisely his imperfection: his humility and his willingness to do the long, inner work of prayer and formation. Evidence abounds pointing to Washington's evolving faith and growing integrity. Others in his time noticed that conversion of heart.

Just 15 days after George Washington's death at Mount Vernon, The Reverend Richard Allen, a Methodist minister and ardent abolitionist who later founded the African Methodist Episcopal Church, preached a eulogy in Washington's honor. [44]

Rev. Allen's words focus on Washington as a lifelong slave owner. Yet Allen did not detract from Washington's character. On the contrary, he praised his compassion, courageous struggle, and integrity.

Allen noted that the nation was mourning, in a *"season of festivity,"* for the man he called *"Our father and friend."* Allen also told his congregants they had a special, *"particular cause to bemoan our loss."* He said Washington had been:

> *"a sympathizing friend and tender father"* who had *"watched over us, and viewed our degraded and afflicted state with compassion and pity – his heart was not insensible to our sufferings. He whose wisdom the nations revered thought we had a right to liberty. Unbiased by the popular opinion of the state in which is the memorable Mount Vernon – he dared to do his duty, and wipe off the stain with which man could ever reproach him."*

Allen went on to praise Washington as a man who *"did not fight for that liberty which he desired to withhold from others,"* but instead *"let the oppressed go free"* and *"undid every burden."*

Allen's eulogy was alluding to a provision that Washington placed upon the executors in his last will and testament. In his will, Washington had demanded the emancipation of all the slaves that had belonged to him, upon the occasion of Martha Washington's death. Ironically, Rev. Allen's eulogy was the only eulogy that directly alluded to Washington's emancipation of Mount Vernon's enslaved people.

Remarking further upon that provision, Rev. Allen concluded:

"deeds like these are not common" and that "God would openly reward such acts of beneficence." He predicted: "the name of Washington will live when the sculptured marble and the statue of bronze shall be crumbled into dust – for it is the decree of the eternal God that 'the righteous shall be had in everlasting remembrance."[45]

The great churchman, family man, farmer, General, and President was eulogized no fewer than 400 times – and by people of different faiths. Washington was a Christian with a broad acceptance of others' religious traditions.

Nevertheless, Washington's grave marker contains a Christian burial hymn from the Anglican 1662 Book of Common Prayer. Washington used the Book of Common Prayer in private prayer and corporate worship all his life.

On his original tomb are etched these words, which are familiar to every Anglican through the ages, from the Book of Common Prayer's Order for the Burial of the Dead:

"I AM the resurrection and the life, saith the Lord: he that believeth in me, though he were dead, yet shall he live: and whosoever liveth and believeth in me shall never die." (John 11:25-26)

The rest of that burial hymn says:

"I know that my Redeemer liveth, and that he shalt stand at the latter day upon the earth. And though my skin worms destroy this body, yet in my flesh shall I see God: whom I sall see for myself, and mine eyes shall behold, and not another." (Job 19:25)

"WE brought nothing into this world, and it is certain we carry nothing out. The Lord gave, and the Lord hath taken away. Blessed be the name of the Lord." (1 Timothy 6:7 and Job 1:21) [46]

During the French and Indian War, soldiers reported that Washington had read the same Burial Hymn from the Book of Common Prayer, as he led an impromptu burial service for General Edward Braddock.

The regular practice of prayer (according to one's own tradition) and the quest for moral integrity were hallmarks of Washington's formation. He believed being spiritually grounded was the path to both personal and national joy.

Washington was convinced that a nation devoid of prayer, one that placed restrictions on freedom, or that engaged in division that polarizes, would never experience *"Happiness."*

The pinnacle of George's lasting spiritual legacy is his insistence that both personal and national joy, or *"Happiness,"* must be rooted and grounded in prayerful union with God and others. During his presidency and his golden years, Washington often used the Eucharistic phrase, *"Cup of Blessing"* to describe this sense of joy, which he called *"happiness."*

Yet, Washington's sense of joy was tempered over time by the experience of God in the midst of sorrow as well.

Washington's spiritual formation was influenced by the Anglican theology and latitudinarian ethos he experienced at Pohick Church for dozens of years. His 23 years on Pohick' Vestry helped shape him into the leader he would eventually become.

Over his lifetime, Washington faced many of life's greatest challenges – more than some of us will ever experience. Yet, as he remained grounded in prayer, in humble self-reflection, and in openness to his own transformation, Washington gradually embraced a balanced, wise, and mature trust in *the inscrutable ways of Providence"* -- regardless of life's circumstances.

Exploring Washington's journey makes his legacy more accessible, relatable, and inspiring. For Washington's imperfections and his lifelong process of struggle, transformation, and growth mirror our own.

Most people do not achieve the heights of perfection, even in a lifetime.

Yet, in choosing to follow a spiritual path, one can re-adjust focus, name imperfections, notice God present in both sorrows and blessings, and surrender to being changed.

Like Washington, everyone can choose to be prayerful and intentional about a lifelong process of transformation and growth. By embarking on a spiritual path to joy, every human being has the God-given, grace-filled potential to bring beliefs in line with actions – and ultimately experience integrity.

As people and nations embrace the mystery of God present in all of life -- and in time, learn to trust in Providence's inscrutable ways -- they may just encounter that deep-seated well of joy and hope that George Washington described as *"Happiness."*

9

Images

POHICK CHURCH
COME FOR THE HISTORY; STAY FOR THE WORSHIP!
THE VERY REV DR. LYNN RONALDI, RECTOR
SUNDAY WORSHIP   8 AM & 10:30 AM
CHRISTIAN EDUCATION AND FELLOWSHIP   9:15 AM
COMPLETED 1774:   WWW.POHICK.ORG
DOCENT TOURS AVAILABLE   ALL WELCOME

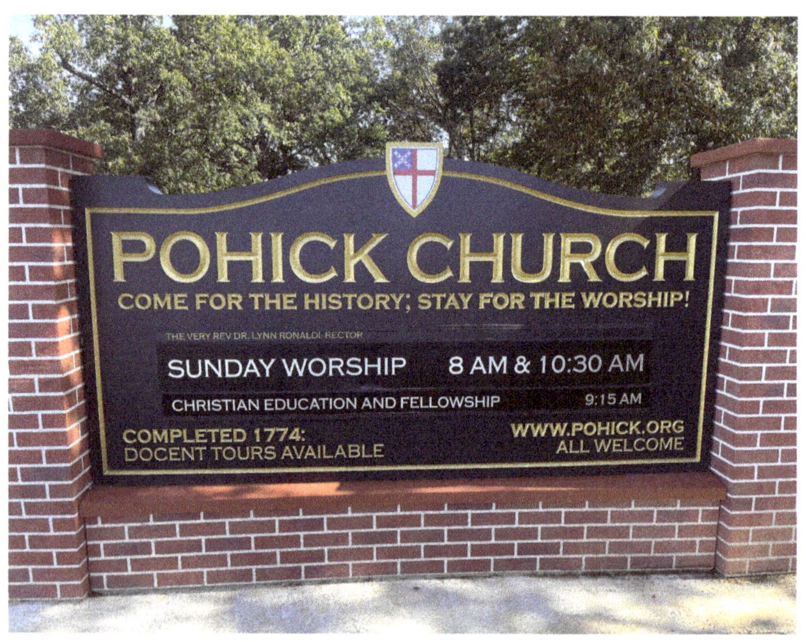

Pohick Church as it stands in 2024.

Inside the current day Pohick Church.

Pohickians view the original 1732 – 1802 Vestry
minutes, on display for the first time in the church during
the annual visit of the Mount Vernon Ladies' Association.

Rev. Lynn Ronaldi presents the original vestry minutes to Mount Vernon CEO Doug Bradburn to preserve, on loan, to the George Washington Presidential Library at Mount Vernon.

Original Pohick Church Vestry
minutes.

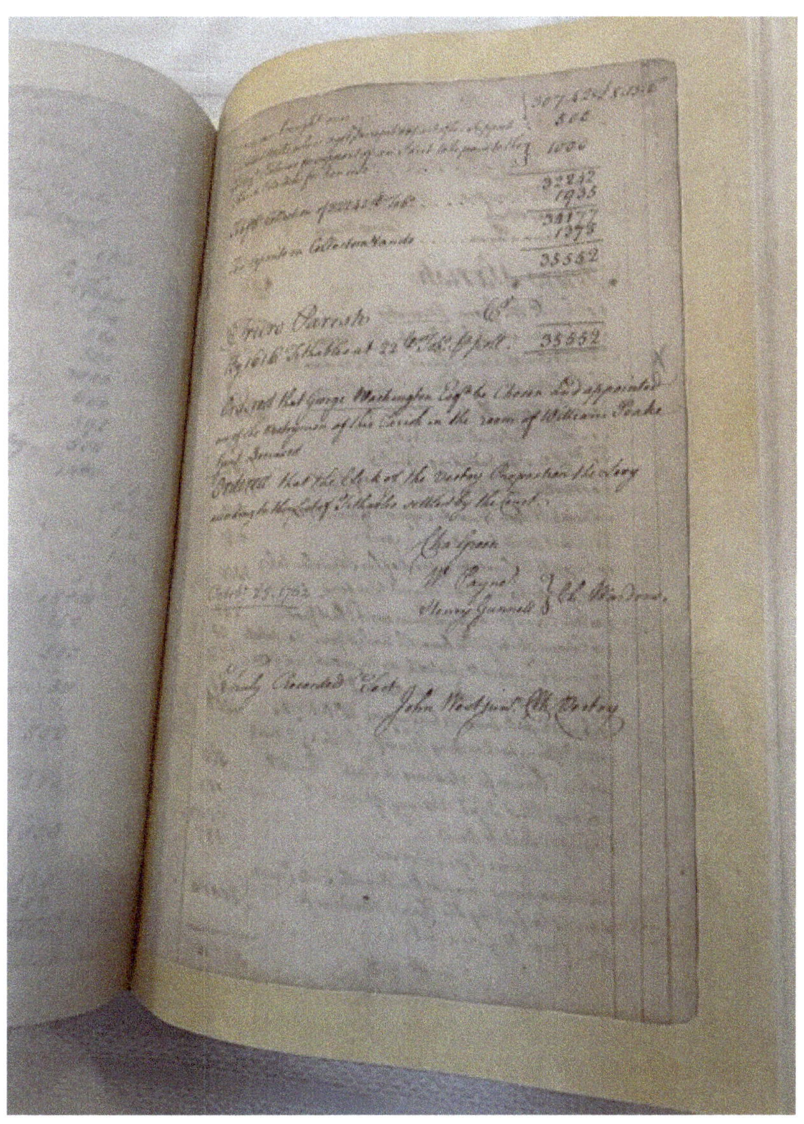

Pohick Vestry Minutes opened to the day that George
Washington was appointed to the Vestry in 1762.

2023 Pohick Vestry views the original 1732-1785 Truro
Parish at Pohick Vestry minutes, which are on loan at the
George Washington Presidential Library and stored in
the General's private publications collection.

Pohick Vestry had its annual retreat at the George
Washington Presidential Library at Mount Vernon in
March, 2023.

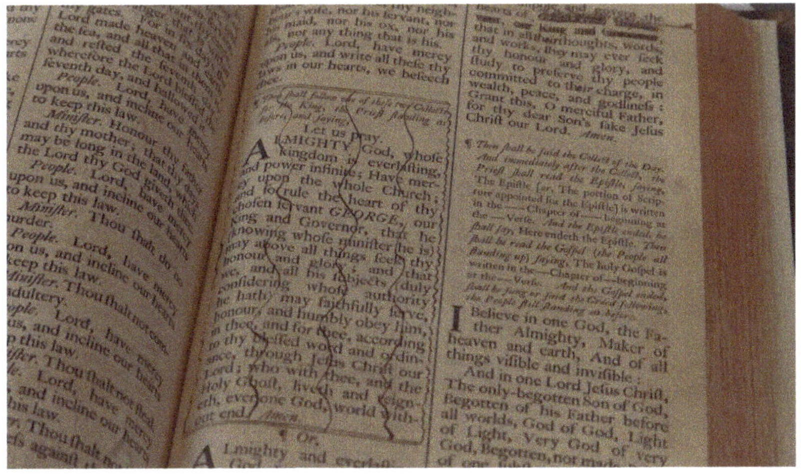

Pohick Church's 1662 Book of Common Prayer ordered
by George Washington in which the prayer for the
Monarch was purged by a predecessor.

Rev. Dr. Lynn Ronaldi participates in the symposium, "Religion in the Age of the American Revolution" alongside Dr. John Fea, Dr. Richard Newman, Dr. Douglas Bradburn, and Dr. Patrick Spero at the Pohick Church 250th Anniversary Grand Celebration At Mount Vernon on February 10, 2024.
Taken by Abigale Wallace Photography, LLC

Pohick Church historic items on display at the 250th Anniversary Grand Celebration At Mount Vernon on February 10, 2024 including the Chapman painting of Pohick Church and the original Vestry minutes.
Taken by Abigale Wallace Photography, LLC

The Chapman Painting
Taken by Abigale Wallace Photography, LLC

Pohick Church's 1662 Book of Common Prayer.
Taken by Abigale Wallace Photography, LLC.

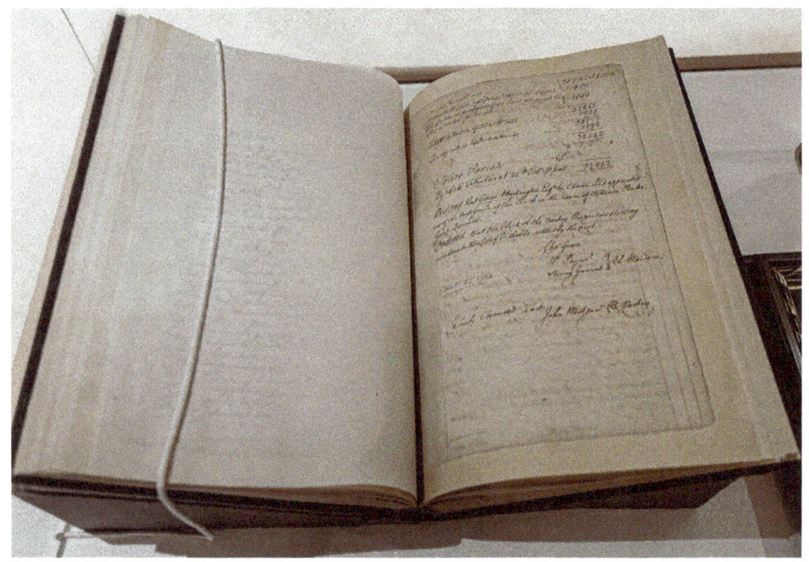

Original Pohick Church Vestry minutes on display at the 250th Jubilee Celebration at Mount Vernon.
Taken by Abigale Wallace Photography, LLC.

Close-up of the Washington family communion chalice.
Taken by Abigale Wallace Photography, LLC

The Mount Vernon Ladies Association
(MVLA), and Mount Vernon CEO
Doug and Nadene Bradburn participate
in Eucharist on the Piazza, at the close
of their annual meeting.
Courtesy Rev. Dr. Lynn Ronaldi

On the Mount Vernon piazza, Rev. Dr.
Lynn Ronaldi lifts Pohick's
Washington family chalice as she
celebrates the Eucharist at the annual
Mount Vernon Ladies' Association
meeting.
Courtesy Rev. Dr. Lynn Ronaldi

The underside of the Washington family silver
communion chalice stamped with dates back to 1737.
Courtesy Rev. Dr. Lynn Ronaldi

Augustine Washington walks with his young son, George Washington.
Mount Vernon Ladies' Association

Washington as a Surveyor / New York G.P. Putnam & Co.
Image courtesy of Mount Vernon Ladies' Association.

Ink and watercolor. George Washington Reading Prayers to his troops in camp.

Image courtesy of Mount Vernon Ladies' Association.

Portrait of General George Washington. Bequest of
Luisita L. Cofer, 1956.
Image courtesy of Mount Vernon Ladies' Association.

Ink on paper by John C. McRae / The Prayer at Valley Forge.
Image courtesy of the Mount Vernon Ladies' Association.

Ink on tin plated iron depicting George Washington's return to Mount Vernon after the Revolutionary War. George Washington is just arriving in the central passage at Mount Vernon, where he greets Martha Washington and a young Nelly Custis.

Courtesy of Mount Vernon Ladies' Association.

Ink on paper rendering of George Washington walking his beloved farm at Mount Vernon.

Image courtesy of Mount Vernon Ladies' Association.

**Ink on paper portraying The Washington Family.
Washington always enjoyed time spent with his family at
Mount Vernon "under his own vine and fig tree."**
Image courtesy of the Mount Vernon Ladies' Association.

Ink on paper Mount Vernon the home of George Washington.
Image courtesy of the Mount Vernon Ladies' Association.

Ink and watercolor print of a view of the Old Tomb of the
Washington family.
Image courtesy of Mount Vernon Ladies' Association.

Appendix

"Answering God's Call to Follow, to Struggle, and to be Transformed"

The Spiritual Witness of Pohick's Ancestors,

Sermon Preached to Pohick Church on its 250th Anniversary, 1/14/24
1 Samuel 3:1-10, Psalm 139, John 1:43-51
The Very Rev. Dr. Lynn P. Ronaldi, Rector of Pohick Church

On this significant occasion, at this commemorative service launching our 250th anniversary in this church, it is tempting to place Pohick's spiritual ancestors on a pedestal.

After all, the likes of George Washington and George Mason and their families, among others, were founding fathers and mothers of our nation. As a result, we tend to regard them as spiritual giants – as perfect models of the faith. Stellar Christians who knew God's voice and immediately uttered a resounding and unequivocal "yes" to God's call.

We might even imagine they precisely discerned the path God wanted them to take. That they perfectly embodied the righteousness and justice of Jesus in their courageous quest for human freedom and equality.

If that's what you imagine, I'm going to burst your bubble. Turn your fantasy into reality. You can believe this: Not one human being aside from Jesus is perfect – not even the Georges.

I submit that their enduring gift to us is in fact their imperfection and their ongoing struggle to know and follow God. Their profound spiritual contribution is their willingness to keep listening, and say "yes" to the long, hard inner work of transformation.

Like many heroes of the faith, they grew over a lifetime. And it was precisely through their struggle that they were transformed. Persevering in prayer and self- reflection, they gradually moved away from naiive certainty and spiritual deafness toward a listening and discerning ear, and acceptance of God's mysterious ways.

Clearly, they are in good company! In all our Scripture readings, Biblical characters struggle to hear God's call and discern his purposes.

Samuel only dimly hears God's voice in the night when God calls him by name. It takes three tries before God finally gets through, and Samuel recognizes who's calling.

When Eli instructs the boy to open his spiritual ears and invite God to speak, Samuel finally says, *"Speak Lord, for your servant is listening."* Although Samuel is not ready, he gradually grows, and trusts the God he cannot fully comprehend.

In Psalm 139, the writer perceives that God intimately knows and loves us, yet we cannot fully know God. While the psalmist senses that God is all-present, all-knowing and all-loving, he recognizes God is unknowable: That God's ways are *"weighty and vast."* So, even when he does not fully apprehend God, in time, he trusts the God who has always known and loved him.

Finally, in John's Gospel, Nathaniel actually encounters God-in-the-flesh, Jesus, and still does not recognize him! Yet, Jesus immediately knows Nathaniel through and through – knowing *"there is no guile"* in Nathaniel. It is Jesus' act of intimate knowing that convinces Nathaniel that Jesus is the *"Son of God."*

In all these stories, not one of these Biblical characters is perfect. Not one of them even recognizes God at first.

Only when God calls them by name, do they comprehend that they are known and loved -in spite of being imperfect. It is in the very midst of their struggle, that learn to hear God's voice. It is their newfound humility and willingness-to-be -changed that sets them on the path to transformation.

And these characters are but a tiny fraction of the thousands of imperfect Biblical characters. All of them lacked something. Not one of them was "ready" to be called. Just look at Jesus' closest disciples. As theologian Ron Rolheiser points out:

- Jesus called skeptical Nathaniel. Nathaniel lacked openness. Nathaniel wasn't ready.

- Jesus called hotheads John and his brother James, the Sons of Thunder. They lacked a sense of servanthood. They were not ready.
- Jesus called Doubting Thomas. Thomas lacked vision. Thomas wasn't ready.
- Jesus called Peter, the Rock. Peter lacked courage. Peter wasn't ready.

And the list goes on – not one of the 12 was perfect. Not one was ready. Yet Jesus called them anyway.

Though none of them knew what they were getting into, they each assented when Jesus said, *"Come and see."* And as they followed Jesus and experienced God's mysterious love and mercy, they were gradually transformed. Their perseverance in the struggle is precisely what makes them spiritual models for us.

Because on any given day, don't most of us walk in chaos and uncertainty? We are unbalanced and inconsistent in our spiritual lives. We experience toxic relationships. We are painfully aware of our own failings and sin.

Yet, God still calls us, for he knows the heart. As they say, "God doesn't call the equipped; God equips the called."

And this is where we can look to Pohick's spiritual ancestors. They were imperfect as well. They all lacked something. They were not ready. Yet God called them, and in time, they listened. They followed the call *to "come and see."* And they were willing to be changed over the span of a lifetime.

All of them struggled and grew. But the one I've come to know best is George Washington. I've spent considerable time studying his life and spiritual formation.

I'm convinced that he was neither a perfect person, nor was he a moral failure. We should neither idolize nor demonize him. I believe Washington's greatest gifts to us were his spiritual and moral struggles, his willingness to be transformed, his dawning trust in what he called *"the inscrutable ways of Providence."*

"Providence" was a word many in his day used for God. Like today's psalmist, Washington gradually came to see that God was unknowable, "inscrutable." But he also came to believe we could trust God's ways, even in the face of suffering and evil.

This trust in God's ways regardless of suffering and pain was not always present in his life. As a youth, he lacked wisdom; his prayer life was proscribed and simple.

As a young man fighting in the French and Indian War, Washington lacked clear vision. He believed in God's presence and action only when things went well for him. When his life was spared, he naiively presumed he was in God's favor.

It was later, as a General of the Continental Army -- when he faced real suffering, sickness, death, and near despair -- that Washington's faith deepened and his wisdom evolved. In the midst of suffering, he persevered in prayer. He ordered his troops to pray, and encouraged them to pray according to their own religious tradition.

During the war years, Washington showed real signs of spiritual transformation. One evidence of the inner struggle and change of heart was his view toward the institution of slavery. He was fighting for the cause of liberty and freedom, and often used the language, *"being freed from the shackles of England."* He could hardly miss the irony of holding human beings in captivity.

Watching the brave soldiers of African descent fight courageously alongside white soldiers, Washington's heart was gradually changed. He integrated his army, no longer separating black from white.

He also began expressing his struggle with slavery and exploring options for abolishing it. He corresponded with abolitionist-leaning friends like Marquis de Lafayette, Alexander Hamilton, and fellow Pohickian George Mason.

Were you aware that the two Georges, Washington and Mason, left Pohick after worship one Sunday in 1774, to ride to Mount Vernon and draft the Fairfax Resolves? Written 250 years ago, the Resolves influenced our Constitution. One of its resolutions specifically addresses the abomination of slavery.

In time, Washington struggled with this institution that was second nature to his time. As President, he came to see that slavery needed to die. He merely struggled with the method of abolishing it – wanting to do so in a measured way that did not divide the newly united colonies. Were it to come to dividing over it, Washington wrote that he would side with the North against slavery. And near the end of his life, Washington decided to free his slaves, through his will.

The more I learn about Washington, the less I appreciate him for his sterling character. On the contrary, I revere him for his very human imperfections, his struggles, his perseverance in prayer, and his humble willingness to listen to God's voice throughout his life, be transformed, and follow God's call with integrity.

Unfortunately, today some persist in demonizing Washington, among other reasons, because he owned slaves. In our "cancel culture," some demonize others when they do not fight a perceived injustice the way they do. They seek to force change.

Today, on the eve of Martin Luther King Day, I wonder if the true essence of Dr. King's teaching was antithetical to demonization and forced change, and more about the process.

D'Andrea, Don and I had the privilege of hearing Dr. Catherine Meeks speak at our recent Diocesan Convention. Executive director of the Absolom Jones Center for Racial Healing, Dr. Meeks is a professor and author known for her lifetime of promoting racial justice.

Dr. Meeks clearly and unequivocally challenges any form of demonization, forced change, or formulas for quick fixes. She writes:

"Much effort has been expended across the years trying to find a magic cure for racism..." She says, "We must approach (Dr. King's) idea of beloved community as a process of making space in the head and the heart so God can enter that space with energy that creates something new."

She also said, *"Don't be out there trying to save everybody else. Start with yourself. Be a pilgrim on the journey to wholeness sand integrity. Do your own inner work of transformation. Own it and face up to it... If you go around being an activist and demanding change your way, you become little tyrants who project their own issues, and alienate others..."*

In her book, Dr. Meeks concludes: *"Beloved community is born when there is a genuine willingness to listen to one's heart, try to discern its call, and commit to finding a path that will allow us to respond to what our heart asks of us."*[47]

No, we are not perfect. Nor can we demand perfection of others, as we see it. All we can do is our own inner work of transformation.

We are not ready. We all lack something. Yet God persists in calling us into a living relationship with Him that changes our hearts. Like Jesus called the imperfect Nathaniel and his other disciples. Like he called the imperfect George Washington and George Mason – like he calls you and me.

As we celebrate the 250th Aynniversary of our church home, let us admire the witness of our spiritual ancestors – not because they are pillars of morality and perfection -- but precisely because they are not. Because they answered the call anyway, and entered into a lifetime process of transformation that formed them into true leaders.

As Dr. Meeks says, *"Be a pilgrim on the journey to wholeness and integrity."*

Do your own work of transformation. Spend time in prayer and self-reflection, and stay in the struggle. You might begin your prayer, saying, *"Speak Lord, for your servant is listening."* And then, when God calls, whether you feel ready or not, answer, *"Here I am Lord. Send me."* Amen.

10

Endnotes

1. ^ *Founders Online webpage, search of" providence" and "trust"*

2. ^ Truro Parish at Pohick Church 1732-1785 Vestry Minutes

3. ^, Henriques, Peter *Realistic Visionary*2006 Virginia Press, p 1x.)

4. ^ Nordham, George Washington, *George Washington's Religious Faith,* Rare Books Collection of GW Presidential Library, Adams Press, Chicago 1986, p. 46

5. ^ Founders Online Search: happy, happiness, joy

6. ^ 1732-1785 Vestry Minutes of Truro Parish at Pohick Church

7. ^ Thompson, Mary, I*n the Hands of a Good Providence,* p 18

8. ^ Ibid, p. 21

9. ^ Pyle, *The Boyle Lectures (1692-173)2, p 1-3*

10. ^ Thompson, Mary, *In the Hands of a Good Providence, p. 22"*

11. ^ Vicchio, Stephen J, *George Washington's Religion, p.101*

12. ^ Founders Online Search, cup of sorrows, suffering, blessing

13. ^ Barton, David, *The Bulletproof George Washington,* vol. 1, 7-18, 1755.

14. ^ Lillback, Peter, *George Washington's Sacred Fire,* c Peter Lillback, 2006, *p 998, endnote 19*

15. ^ 1732-1785 Minutes of Truro Parish at Pohick Church

16. ^ Lillback, Peter, *Sacred Fire,,* p. 597

17. ^Ibid, p. 255

18. ^Thompson, Mary, *In the Hands of a Good Providence*, p. 53

19. ^ Ibid, p 93

20. ^ Ibid, p 94

21. ^ Ibid, p 97

22. ^ Washington, George, Valley Forge Diary, Dec. 12, 1777

23. ^ Vichhio, Stephen, *George Washington's Religion, p. 141*

24. ^ George Washington, Valley Forge, December 12, 1777

25. ^ Vicchio, Stephen, *George Washington's Religion*, p. 141

26. ^ Thompson, Mary, *In the Hands of a Good Providence, p 115*

27. ^ *Founding Fathers Online reference, "Cup of Suffering," "Cup of Sorrows"*

28. ^ Lillback, Peter, *Sacred Fire,* p 433-435

29. ^ Thompson, Mary, *In the Hands of a Good Providence,"* p 148

30. ^ Ibid, p 149

31. ^ Lillback, Peter, *Sacred Fire,* p 358

32. ^ Ibid, p 151

33. ^ Schroeder. J.F., *Maxims of Washington,"* p. 363, c Sept.12, 1854 New York, NY (MVLA special collection)

34. ^ Thompson, Mary, *The Only Unavoidable Subject of Regret,* p 3

35. ^ Ibid, p 68: Thomas Coke, *Extracts of the Journals,* p 45

36. ^ Ibid, p 70

37. ^ Lillback, Peter, *George Washington's Sacred Fire, p. 361*

38. ^ Ibid, p 362

39. ^ Lillback, Peter, *Sacred Fire,* p 433

40. ^ Novak, Michael and Jana, *Washington's God, p 156*

41. ^ Buffington, Joseph, *The Soul of George Washington,"* p. 169, c 1936 Dorrance and Co., Philadelphia

42. ^ Michael and Jana Novak, *Washington's God, p. 239*

43. ^ Thompson, Mary, *The Only Unavoidable Subject of Regret,* p 293

44. ^ Newman, Richard, *Freedom's Prophet, p. 137*

45. ^ Lillback, Peter, *Sacred Fire,* p.356

46. ^ Meeks, Catherine, *The Night is Long, Light Comes in the Morning.*

Bibliography

Barton, David. The Bulletproof George Washington. Vol. 1. 7-18 WallBuilders Press, 1990.

Boyle Lectures 1692-1732, Cambridge University Press, 1-3. Published online by Cambridge.

Buffington, Joseph. The Soul of George Washington. 169-170. Dorrance and Company Publishing, 1936.

Enriques, Peter. Realistic Visionary. x. University of Virginia Press, 2006.

Founders Online. Several searches on author/recipient George Washington. National Archives. https//www.foundersarchives.gov.

Hale, Sir Matthew. Contemplations Moral and Divine. Mary Ball Washington's copy in Special Collection at George Washington Presidential Library. Shrowsbery and Leigh, London, 1685.

Jackson, Donald (editor). Diaries of George Washington. Volume 1-6. U.S. Press, 1967.

Lillback, Peter. George Washington's Sacred Fire. 151, 255, 356, 358, 433-435, 597, 998, Dickinson Press, 2006.

Maguire, E.P. The Religious Opinion and Character of George Washington. Special Collection of George Washington Presidential Library. Harper Brothers, 1836.

Meeks, Catherine. The Night is Long, but Light Comes in the Morning. 157. Morehouse Publishing, 2022.

Newman, Richard. Freedom's Prophet. 136-137. New York University Press, 2008.

Nordham, G.W. George Washington's Religious Faith. 46. Rare Book Collection of George Washington Presidential Library. Adena Press, Chicago. 1986.

Novak, Michael and Jana. Washington's God. 156, 238. Basic Books, 2006.

Pohick Church, Minutes of the Vestry, Truro Parish at Pohick Church 1735-1785. Gateway Press, 1995.

Schroeder, J.F. Maxims of George Washington. 363. MVLA Rare Books Collection of George Washington Presidential Library, 1854.

Thompson, Mary. In the Hands of a Good Providence. 18, 21, 53, 93, 94, 97, 115, 148, 149. University of Virginia Press, 2008.

Thompson, Mary. The Only Unavoidable Subject of Regret. 3, 68, 70, 293, 362. University of Virginia Press, 2019.

Vicchio, Stephen. George Washington's Religion. 101, 139-143. Wipf and Stock Publishers, 2019.

Washington, George. Valley Forge Diary. Dec. 12, 1777.

About the Author

The Rev. Dr. Lynn Ronaldi is an Episcopal priest who was 16th Rector of Pohick Church in the Diocese of Virginia. Recently retired from full-time parish ministry, she was Pohick's first female Rector in its nearly 300-year history. She also served as Dean of the Potomac Region, appointed by the Bishop of Virginia.

During the time she was researching this book, the author was delighted to learn through genealogist Stephen McCleod, that her own family is descended from Maryland House of Burgesses Representative James Smallwood. In the 17th century, he proposed legislation to legalize Protestantism in Maryland. Through this ancestor she became a Colonial Dame of the Washington DC Chapter.

She and her husband Tom live in a mountain home in Jasper Highlands, Tennessee. There she enjoys easy access to their two youngest daughters: a nurse recruiter and a teacher, in Chattanooga. Their oldest is a fellow in vascular surgery at Mayo Clinic.

She and Tom live "one mountain over" from Sewanee's School of Theology. A Certified Spiritual Director and CPE Supervisor, Ronaldi participates in the formation of seminarians at Sewanee. She continues to write; provide spiritual direction; and celebrate, preach, and counsel where called.

Ronaldi earned her MDiv from St. Mary's Seminary in Houston in 2013. In 2016, she earned a Doctor of Ministry (DMin) from the Sewanee School of Theology. Her doctoral thesis *Towards a Spiritual Formation Model of Clinical Pastoral Education* created a new approach to clinical pastoral education (CPE), by integrating Benedictine spirituality into the CPE model. Rev. Lynn also holds a BA in Journalism from Ole Miss, and an MBA from The University of Dallas. She is a Board-Certified Chaplain, Pastoral Counselor, and Diplomate CPE Supervisor for CPSP; and IMN certified. In her free time, Ronaldi enjoys time with family; reading and writing about theology and contemplative spirituality; reading fiction and listening to stories; and hiking, needlework, and traveling.